The Illustrated Guide

TO THE

GREAT WESTERN RAILWAY.

BY

GEORGE MEASOM.

Embellished with Fifty Illustrations from Original Drawings.

LONDON:

PUBLISHED BY W. MARSHALL AND SONS,

BOOKSELLERS TO THE COMPANY,

PADDINGTON STATION.

NOTICE.

Mr. George Measom has in a forward state of progress an Official Illustrated Guide to the

SOUTH EASTERN RAILWAY,

(*LONDON BRIDGE TO PARIS;*)

and the

BRIGHTON RAILWAY.

The latter will include graphic descriptions of everything connected with the Crystal Palace.

Both Books will be beautifully Illustrated from original Drawings made for the purpose.

First published 1852

This facsimile edition published by Berkshire County Library
in association with
Countryside Books 1985

No reproduction of this edition permitted without the prior permission of Berkshire County Library.

Produced through MRM (Print Consultants) Ltd., Reading.

Countryside Books, 3 Catherine Road, Newbury, Berkshire.

List of Illustrations

BY GEORGE MEASOM.

Contents.

The Illustrated Guide

GREAT WESTERN RAILWAY.

INTRODUCTION.

THE Great Western Railway was suggested, in the first instance, by the anxious desire of the merchants and men of influence in Bristol, as well as of the colliery-owners and clothing-manufacturers of Gloucestershire and Somersetshire, in order to establish for themselves the same rapid and effective communication with the Metropolis which had already been secured under Act of Parliament for Liverpool, Manchester, and Birmingham. In practice, however, it has proved, that neither to the shipping-trade of Bristol, nor to its neighbouring coal-fields, nor to the manufacturing industry of Gloucester, Somerset, and Wilts, does this great Line owe its present success and prosperity; for the importance of Bristol, as a commercial port, as far at least as regards a portion of its exports, has yearly diminished, owing to the constantly rising importance of Liverpool and Glasgow; the collieries of West Somerset and South Gloucestershire are neither now nor ever can be valuable, except to the neighbourhood in which they lie; and the clothiers of the West have been all but superseded in the markets by the great manufacturers of the West-Riding of Yorkshire. Commerce, indeed, and manufacturing industry and inland-trade, have undoubtedly furnished staple materials for the vast business of the London and Birmingham Railway, and its continuations; but the Great Western owes its chief success, and the success, also, of its adjunct and dependent lines, to a distinct section of the population altogether,—in fact, to that portion of the people of England who possess the property of the soil, are supported by its produce, or derive their subsistence from supplying the wants of the landowners, their tenants, and their labourers. This, at least, has been the case down to the present time; though it seems more than probable, that the early opening of the Branch-line through Oxford and Banbury to Birmingham, in order to compete with the London and North Western, will introduce the Great Western to a new source of traffic and revenue among the manufacturing interest, of which the Birmingham and Manchester Lines have hitherto enjoyed so long a monopoly.

The success of the Great Western Railway, notwithstanding its grand scale, and all the vastly additional expense of its construction and maintenance, is positive and permanent; nor need we wonder at it, when we recollect, that this great Trunk-line itself (exclusive of the Bristol and Exeter, the South Devon, and the South Wales Branch-lines) forms a channel of communication with such places as the following:—

	Population.		Population.
Bristol and Clifton (1851)...	143,700	Windsor and Eton..............	40,890
Bath........................	69,840	Banbury	29,790
Cheltenham..................	40,246	Chippenham	21,420
Stroud	37,380	Cirencester	21,330
Gloucester..................	32,060	Newbury	20,820
Devizes	22,240	Hungerford	20,410
Reading.....................	22,170	Oxford.......................	20,170

Let us add to these about thirty other towns, having more than 10,000 inhabitants; and we shall have a merely *civic* population of about *twelve hundred thousand;* to which, if we add again about 900,000 for the rural population of South Bucks, Berks, West Oxfordshire, North Wiltshire, Somersetshire, and Gloucestershire, we shall have a grand total of about *two millions* of persons, living in the provinces, who receive benefit, either directly or indirectly, from the establishment and maintenance of the Great Western. To these, again, we must add that vast but undefinable number of persons, who use this Line as the medium of their pleasures, as a rapid means of access to some pleasant spot, chosen for a holiday's trip,—to some meeting of hounds,—to some secluded stream loved by anglers, &c. &c. ; and, once more, we must not forget to take into our calculation the numbers of the inhabitants of London constantly using the Line for short journeys into the suburbs, and likewise the great influx of travellers from many and various quarters, who, having travelled long distances on the narrow gauge of other Lines, are glad to get quickly home by the broad gauge of the Great Western Company. On the whole, therefore, we are not far from the mark, when we say, that a population of nearly *three millions* of people avail themselves, directly or indirectly, of the immense advantages offered by the Great Western Railway, for conveying not only various classes of passengers, but every description of luggage.

The first idea of this most important Line was published to the world in the local reports of a great meeting held at Bristol, July 30, 1833; the result of which was, the formation of a Company of Shareholders, with a capital not exceeding £2,500,000 sterling. The first application for a Bill to Parliament was made in 1834, (William IV. 4 and 5,) simply for powers to construct Lines between London and Reading, and between Bristol and Bath ; but, although it passed the Commons, it was lost in the House of Lords. In the following Session, however, (1835,) another and more extended Bill was offered for the sanction of Parliament,—intended, as its preamble declares, " for the purpose of improving the existing communication between the Metropolis, the Western districts of England, the South of Ireland, and Wales ;"— and this Bill, with certain modifications, was finally made into a law through the exertions of the late Lord Wharncliffe, the Chairman of the Lords' Committee, and Charles Russell, Esq., (son of the late Sir Charles Russell, of Swallowfield Place, near Wokingham,) who was at that time Member for Reading, and Chairman of the Commons' Committee. This Act dates August 31, 1835 ; and, owing to the great and ludicrously violent opposition it met with from the landholders, the parliamentary expenses reached very nearly to £90,000. At the same time, the cost of purchasing land, and money paid for compensation, amounted to £6,300 per mile, while the expense of construction averaged about £47,000 per mile; thus involving an expense for the permanent way, quite independently of the rolling stock, amounting to upwards of six millions sterling.

The Great Western Railway, as is well known, differs from all others, in being constructed on the *broad gauge principle;*—that is, its rails are *seven feet* instead of *four feet nine inches* apart. Hence, therefore, the locomotive-engines on that Line are of a peculiar construction, and great size, in order to adapt them to so large a gauge, and they have also a short quick stroke of the piston, as compared with the size of the driving-wheels. They run for the most part on six wheels, with driving-wheels seven feet in diameter; and the weight of the engine, with its fuel and water, is equivalent to nineteen tons, exercising a power of 120 horses, supposed to work at the rate of forty-five miles an hour. At the same time its tender, running on six wheels, carries twenty-five hundred weight of coke, and 1,600 gallons of water; the length of the engine and tender together being about forty feet. It may be desirable, also, to mention, that the weight of a first-class carriage, with thirty-two passengers, amounts to $7\frac{1}{2}$ tons; that of a second-class, $7\frac{1}{4}$ tons. More recently, however, it has been found desirable to increase the weight and power of the engines. "The Lord of the Isles," for instance, a noble engine on eight wheels, which our readers may remember to have seen at the Great Exhibition, is capable of taking a passenger-train of 120 tons, at an average speed of sixty miles an hour; and its effective power, as ascertained by the dynamometer, is equal to that of 740 horses. Its weight, when in working order, amounts to thirty-five tons, independently of the tender, which, when laden, weighs nearly eighteen more. Its cylinder has a diameter of eighteen, and the piston a stroke of twenty-four inches; while the driving-wheel is eight feet in diameter, and the maximum pressure of steam equal to 120lb. on the square inch. The consumption of coke, also, with a load of twenty tons, travelling thirty miles an hour, amounts to 20lb. per mile. The broad gauge engines, moreover, are extremely costly, averaging not less than £3,000 each, an increase of at least one-third on those made for narrow gauge Railways.

As the relative merits of the BROAD AND NARROW GAUGES have been so long before the public, it will naturally be expected that some observations should be made on the relative speed of the two classes of Railway. The Great Western express trains, starting from London (9.45), including time lost for refreshments at Swindon, and an extra number of stoppages amounting to 29 per cent. not made by the North Western, travel almost at 11 per cent. higher speed than the express trains of the rival Railway; while, were the stoppages made equal, the speed on the Great Western would be $25\frac{1}{2}$ per cent. higher; or, in other words, the Great Western express trains would travel, exclusively of time lost in stopping and starting, and while the trains are in a state of rest, at the rate of somewhat more than 55 miles an hour; or including all stoppages at the rate of 42 miles an hour. It must be remembered, also, that while most of the North Western express trains carry only first class passengers, *all* the Great Western expresses carry both first and second class passengers.

The Great Western mail trains, with 37 per cent. more stoppages, and refusing no description of traffic whatever, have only 5 per cent. less speed than the express mails of the North Western ; but supposing the stoppages were equal, the Great Western would still carry second class carriages with rather more than 8 per cent. higher speed. It must be remembered, also, that the speed of the mixed and ordinary trains, with 25 per cent. additional stoppages, is 4 per cent. higher than the ordinary trains on the North Western ; and, supposing the two Lines had equal stoppages, the speed of this would be 20 per cent. more than that of the North Western.

There can be no doubt, therefore, that the Gauge Commissioners were fully justified in giving a favourable verdict as respects speed for the Railway we are now describing ; and it must be only a matter of surprise to all persons acquainted with the evidence, that the said Commissioners, in the face almost of facts known to themselves, and certainly against the strongest professional testimony, gave a general verdict on the ground of mere expediency in behalf of the narrow gauge system.

As respects the traffic on the Great Western we merely observe, that during the first and *worst* half of the present year (1852) the passenger traffic amounted to :—

FIRST CLASS	257,325
SECOND CLASS	1,243,014
THIRD CLASS	354,349
SOLDIERS	9,341
TOTAL	1,864,029

With respect to the PADDINGTON TERMINUS, it must be observed, that everything there is at present (September, 1852) in a state of mutation ; so that no opinion can be formed of its future grandeur or appearance, as compared with the other termini of the Metropolis. None of the present booking-offices, waiting-rooms, platforms, &c., of this great Line, have ever from the first been more than temporary ; but in a few months there will be all the conveniences and appendages of as fine a terminus as London can boast of. Details of all these improvements will be accurately furnished, with appropriate illustrations, in our next edition.

The Hotel at the London Terminus has been built from the designs of Philip Hardwick, Esq., and is not only most advantageously situated in the immediate neighbourhood of Hyde Park and Kensington Gardens, but may be regarded also as one of the finest specimens of modern architecture in the Metropolis. It may be reached by strangers arriving from the Railway, by a covered gallery leading directly from the platform, without the necessity of an intermediate conveyance. The building comprises, also, besides the usual arrangements of a first-rate Hotel, suites of elegant apartments for families, a spacious Coffee-room, Reading-room, Smoking and Billiard-rooms, Hot and Cold Baths, &c. ; besides which, it is proposed to appropriate a portion of the building to the purposes of a Club, for the use of country members, as well as residents in the locality.

ENGINE-HOUSE,　　　　PADDINGTON.

CHAPTER I.

APPROACHES TO THE TERMINUS—TYBURN AND ITS GALLOWS—THE NEW ROAD AND MARYLEBONE GARDENS—INCREASE IN THE POPULATION AND PROSPERITY OF LONDON—PADDINGTON AND ITS HISTORY—WESTBOURN GREEN—GENERAL DESCRIPTION OF THE COUNTRY TRAVERSED—GEOLOGICAL DETAILS.

THE METROPOLITAN STATION of the GREAT WESTERN RAILWAY is situated, as all the world knows, in the parish of Paddington, at the north-west extremity of London, in a locality which, though comprising only green fields forty years ago, is now for the most part covered with fine squares, and noble, spacious streets, erected under leases from the see of London, to which, or to the abbey of Westminster, the manor of Paddington has belonged since the time of Edgar, our Anglo-Saxon monarch in the eighth century. The Terminus is approached by two great lines of thoroughfare, well known to all who have ever visited London,—namely, OXFORD STREET and the EDGEWARE ROAD, from the more central parts of London; and the long line of the NEW ROAD, which skirts the north of the metropolis from FINSBURY SQUARE to the Edgeware Road, not far from the station.

The former of these thoroughfares, which received its present name from the circumstance of its forming the commencement of the great coach-road to *Oxford* through High Wycombe, was, till the beginning of the last century, called the *Tyburn Road*, because it led westward from St. Giles's Pound and Hog Lane (the present Crown Street, Soho,) across Tyburn Brook, which ran through Berkeley Square and May Fair to the large open space, once familiar to the lovers of criminal horrors as the celebrated TYBURN, where, down to 1786, the great malefactors of the metropolis expiated their crimes on the gallows. We have no relish for the annals of human turpitude; but those who are curious in such matters may be glad to know that the Tyburn gallows (which tradition reports to have occupied the site of the present Connaught Place) ridded the world, among many hundred other criminals, of John Felton, the assassin of Villiers, Duke of Buckingham; of Plunket, Archbishop of Armagh, an alleged traitor to the Protestant cause in Ireland; of those celebrated knights of the road and housebreakers, Jack Sheppard, Jonathan Wild, and John Rann, alias "Sixteen-string Jack;" of Lord Ferrers, who murdered his steward, and Dr. Dodd, the forger. The neighbourhood, however, has long been more

B

profitably occupied by streets and squares, some of which may almost vie with aristocratic Belgravia.

The New Road, which forms the other great approach to our Railroad Station, and is altogether about 3½ miles long, including what is now termed the City Road, appears to have been formed soon after the year 1765, not quite ninety years ago; but for several years afterwards it was little better than an ill-kept country road, flanked by fields and market-gardens; nor did it assume any resemblance to its present street-like form till the early part of the present century, when Somer's Town and the Regent's Park district was formed on the site of the old Marylebone Park, whither thrifty tradesmen took their wives and little-ones to enjoy an afternoon at the tea-gardens of the "Adam and Eve," (still existing as a public-house,) and the once favourite resort called the "Jew's Harp." Marylebone Gardens, which stood westward of the New Marylebone church, existed in its full glory, as a fashionable sort of Vauxhall, for more than a century down to 1778; and hundreds of persons are now living, who recollect that by far the larger part of the New Road, west of Tottenham Court Road, was flanked by palings on the northern side as far as Lisson Grove, where the village of Paddington commenced.

Interesting, however, as are these dottings of the past, we feel a far greater pleasure, as we ride onward in our Railway-omnibus, at beholding on both sides of us, northwards as well as southwards, the many unmistakeable proofs of London's progress and prosperity in the numerous streets and squares of its important district, inhabited by the richest of her merchants and the noblest of England's aristocracy; nor can we help citing those lines of the poet Cowper:

> "———— Opulent, enlarged, and still
> Increasing London! Babylon of old
> Not more the glory of the earth than she,
> A more accomplish'd world's chief glory now."

And now, having brought our readers to the immediate neighbourhood of the Terminus, we shall content ourselves with briefly mentioning, that the old parish-church of Paddington, a plain brick building of no architectural pretensions, was, till a comparatively late period, only a chapel-of-ease to St. Margaret's, Westminster; and so humble and uninstructed were the parishioners, that one of the incumbents actually procured ordination for his own porter, that he might fulfil the pastoral duties of this place of worship! How changed are the times now, when, besides the parish-church above mentioned, Paddington has four elegant modern-built Churches, and upwards of a dozen Dissenting Chapels; besides National, Subscription, and Sunday Schools, furnishing religious instruction to more than six thousand of the rising generations!

It may not be without interest, too, if we state, that within half-a-mile of the station there was 30 years ago a pretty retired spot, covered with rural villas, occupied by the late Lord Hill, Mrs. Siddons, and other celebrities,—yclept Westbourn Green,—all now laid out in streets, roads, &c. *St. Mary's Hospital*, also, a handsome red-brick structure, not long built, lies close to the entrance down the Bishop's Road.

The Paddington Terminus, which till the present time has only been fitted up in a temporary manner, and without the proper conveniences for a large and constantly-increasing traffic, promises ere long to equal, if not excel in grandeur of appearance and completeness of accommodation, all the other great termini of London; and the new Hotel is a noble specimen of architecture on a very large scale. As these matters, however, have already been discussed in the brief History of the Great Western Railway, which forms the Introduction to this work, the reader need not be further delayed, but at once conducted to the busy platform, where porters and guards are hurrying to and fro, opening carriage-doors, stowing lugagge, and giving other unmistakeable signs of approaching departure, not a little confirmed by the impatient cries of the fiery, puffing monster, waiting with his driver at the head of the train.

Presuming, however, that the reader of these pages has, like a prudent man, arrived in ample time, and some to spare, for his journey, and as every intelligent traveller is naturally desirous of knowing something about the country he is to traverse, we shall beg him, while he patiently sits in his carriage awaiting the instant of departure, to read the few following remarks on the topographical and geological features of the several counties through which the Great Western extends its iron arms.

If the gentle reader will look over a map of this portion of the country, he will see at a glance that he is about to pass up one great river-valley, and over a dividing elevation or watershed into another, but smaller, river-valley, leading, like the one he has left, to a great and important estuary, the recipient of vast wealth imported to us from foreign countries: in other words, he is about to ascend the Thames-valley, and, after traversing the elevated plains to the north of Marlborough Downs, will gradually slide down into the rich and picturesque valley of the Avon, along which he will pursue his course to Bristol—the busy mart and river-port of the West. From the Metropolis to Maidenhead the Line runs nearly due west over a level plain about five miles north of the Thames, which it crosses at the latter place, and then leaves it till it again meets that river at the important town of Reading, where, as Drayton sang,—

> " ———— once arriv'd, clear Kennet overtakes
> Her lord, the stately Thames;"

and here originates the Branch Line, running about sixteen miles to Newbury and Hungerford, in the valley of the Kennet.

From this point the Line runs for about thirteen miles very close to the river, sometimes on one bank, sometimes another, as far as the Wallingford Road Station; nor does it entirely leave its neighbourhood till beyond Steventon, when it begins rapidly to ascend towards the high lands north of Lambourn and Marlborough Downs, which are distinctly seen to the south between Didcot and Swindon. At the former of these places the Railway sends off a northern branch to Oxford and Banbury,—at the latter a longer one over the Coteswold hills to Gloucester and Cheltenham. The summit level is reached at the eighty-third mile, a little beyond Wootton-Bassett; seven miles beyond which it makes a very rapid descent into the upper valley of " Bath's clear Avon," to which it runs parallel as far as Chippenham (the point of departure for the Wilts and Somerset Branch), and then once more ascends on its way to Corsham and Box Tunnel, down which latter it descends by a rapid incline of fifty-two feet per mile; soon after which it crosses the Avon at Bathford, thence running on its left bank to the entrance of Bath. On leaving that city the Line again crosses the Avon, and thence, nearly to Bristol, keeps pretty close to the south bank, running for seven miles through a district of fine meadow land. At Keynsham, however, the aspect of the scenery entirely changes; and the Railway enters a tract of rugged, precipitous rocks, through which it has to penetrate by means of tunnels and open galleries cut in the coal-strata of the Bristol basin. This wild district passed, the Line enters on an open valley, and, after crossing the Avon for the fifth time, traverses a plain leading to Bishop's Mead, an eastern suburb of Bristol, where the Main Line terminates.

As respects the geological features of the country about to be traversed, it may be remarked generally, that the Railway, as it proceeds westward, passes from the new and upper, to the older and lower groups of rocks, which rise one after another to the surface in a nearly regular order, till we reach the coal-measures at Bristol. In order, however, that the following remarks may be better understood, we shall subjoin a list of the leading tertiary and secondary rocks, down to and including the coal-formations :—

TERTIARY.

Sands and gravels, with marine and fresh water shells.

London clay, containing septaria.

Plastic clay, with sea-shells, plants, &c.

SECONDARY.

Upper chalk, with flint in layers.

Lower chalk, compact, with few flints.

Chalk marl, soft and clayey.

Upper green sand.

Gault, soft, marly clay.

Lower green, or iron sand.

Wealden clay and Hastings sands.

Oolite series—

    Portland or upper oolite.

    Kimmeridge clay.

    Coralline oolite, or Oxford rag.

    Oxford clay.

    Cornbrash and forest marble.

    Great oolite.

    Fuller's earth.

    Lower oolite.

Lias shale and lias limestone.

New red-sandstone.

Upper coal-formations.

The London clay, mostly covered with gravel, forms the groundwork of the line from the Paddington Terminus as far as West Drayton; beyond which it runs as far as Maidenhead through the beds known to geologists as the plastic clay, which is made practically useful in extensive brick-works near Drayton for the supply of the metropolis. At Maidenhead, where the Line first crosses the Thames, we shall traverse the upper chalk beds, though only for a short distance; for before arriving at Reading the tertiary strata are again visible, as at Sonning cutting, a little west of Twyford. From Reading, westward, the Railway gradually traverses the great chalk range of England that extends from Newmarket in Cambridgeshire to the neighbourhood of Devizes; and at Pangbourne cutting, west of the station of that name, the curious observer may see thick beds of chalk, interlaid with flints, which, further on, at Goring cuttings, he will find exchanged for the lower and more compact chalk, almost wholly without flints. After crossing the Thames for the third and last time, at Moulsford bridge, the Great Western enters the chalk-marl beds, abounding with fossils, &c., as may be well seen in the Cholsey Hill cutting, a mile or so west of Moulsford Station. At Didcot the Railway enters (as it were, in the absence of the upper greensand) on a stratum of gault or Tetsworth clay, lying next below the chalk-marl; and in the immediate neighbourhood of the Line, to the northwest, are large beds of lower greensand. The Kimmeridge clay and coral rag are traversed successively between Shrivenham and Chippenham; and a little west of the latter we enter on what are termed the *regular oolitic rocks*, beginning with cornbrash and forest-marble, both of which may be viewed in successive layers at Corsham Station. The Box Tunnel traverses in succession the great or middle (sometimes called *upper*) oolite, so well-known as the Bath building-stone; then two thick beds of fuller's earth and light clay; afterwards the lower or lesser oolite; and lastly, a blue marl-stone or shale, separating the oolites from the lias immediately beneath. In the Avon valley the Railway takes its course through thin beds of blue marl covering the lias; and this, with the occasional appearance of the lower oolite and the fuller's earth stratum above it, constitutes the chief feature of the ground for about eight miles below Bath. As respects the city of Bath itself, it may be briefly remarked, that its lower part, including Pulteney Street, the Abbey Close, and the Pump Rooms, stands on lias covered in general with alluvium, and that the streets and terraces, as they ascend on each side of the Avon, stand successively on the lower oolite and fuller's earth; while the great oolite caps the surrounding eminences of Claverton and Coombe Downs, on the south; of Land Down, Charlcomb Down, and Salisbury northward; and may be traced into Gloucestershire, forming the crowning material of the Cotswold hills to the east of Cheltenham. Two miles west of Bath the Twerton Tunnel penetrates into the new red-sandstone immediately below the lias; but with this exception the lias is the only rock that occurs till beyond Keynsham, where it enters the coal-formation by a small natural defile, in the upper part of which the coal-seams are visible to the passing traveller; and here, for about two miles, the Railroad pursues its course through the sandstone of the coal, which here forms the material on and through which numerous galleries and tunnels are formed in this portion of the Line. The last two miles are over a level surface, composed of the new red-sandstone which forms the substratum of the alluvial plain of Bristol.

From what has been stated, therefore, it will be found that the country traversed by the Great Western Railway, and the districts on each side of it, furnish an ample field for the investigations of the geological student, who wishes to study the various strata of England from its diluvial beds downwards to the coal-formations.

CHAPTER II.

Kensal Green and its Cemetery—Acton and Henry Fielding—Ealing and Gunnersbury—Hanwell and its Asylum—Southall, West Drayton, Hillingdon, and Uxbridge—Langley Park, Ritching's Lodge—Slough—Herschell's House—Stoke-Pogis—The Poet Gray and Sir Edward Coke—Windsor, its Castle and Parks—Eton and Datchet—Runnymede and Magna Charta.

SLOWLY at first, and then more rapidly, the train emerges with its fiery Pegasus from the Terminus, through a neighbourhood surrounded with fourth and fifth-rate houses, occupying the immediate vicinity of the Harrow Road, which, as well as the once busy Paddington Canal (constructed in 1801), runs nearly parallel to the Line for the first two miles. The only objects worthy of mention here, are the new Paddington Workhouse, the Lock Asylum, and the Great Western Company's Gas-works; all on the north side, but none in any way remarkable for their architectural beauty. Ere the first mile, however, has been accomplished, we shall have approached the region of green fields; and looking northward * we shall get a glimpse, distant indeed, of Hampstead

* The editor here begs to inform his readers that, in all possible cases, he will use the term *north* and *south* to indicate the position of objects seen from the Railway; because the terms *right* and *left*, mostly used in such books, must vary with the traveller's position or the way he is travelling, an objection to which the mode of indicating here adopted is not subject.

and Hendon, both well-known and favoured localities with cockney-excursionists and seekers of health.

A mile further, and still on the north side (the right of one looking westward), the Great Western skirts

KENSAL GREEN CEMETERY,

the *Père-la-Chaise* of Western London. This extensive necropolis, which extends over 54 acres, and is flanked on its north side by the North-Western Railway, was only opened about nineteen years ago, and is already becoming pretty full,—convincing proof this of the desirableness of suburban places of sepulture! It contains the remains, too, of many who were celebrated or notorious in their day; as, Lockhart of the *Quarterly Review*, and his friend John Murray, the prince of publishers; Allan Cunningham, the friend and assistant of Chantry; Sydney Smith, the witty "Peter Plymley;" poor "Tom Hood," whose gambols, songs, and "flashes of merriment were wont to set the table on a roar;" Thomas Barnes, the editor of the *Times*; Dr. Birkbeck, the originator of Mechanics' Institutes; and Loudon, the naturalist, with Liston, the far-famed comic-actor; Ducrow, the rider; George Robins, the auctioneer, and two or three celebrities of a more questionable character. Royalty, too, has sought for its ashes a final resting-place within these precincts;—for yonder large granite tomb in front of the chapel contains the remains of the late Duke of Sussex, and his much beloved sister, the Princess Sophia. The patriot duke's example, too, is one day to be followed—but God grant at a very distant one—by our gracious Monarch herself, who has caused a mausoleum to be erected here, in order that she and her race may repose among those with whom they have so long happily and harmoniously gone through life.

Turn we now to the south, and we shall get occasional glimpses, where the embankment will permit, of the elegant and quite modern suburbs of NEW KENSINGTON and NOTTINGHILL, where nearly a thousand acres of green fields have been covered with streets, terraces, and roads lined with detached villas,—not to forget two handsome churches, one

of which has cost upwards of £7,000,—in the incredibly short time of fourteen years! Some of our readers, too, may recollect a portion of the ground as the site of the once well-known Hippodrome, a place for races and rural *fêtes* about a quarter of a century ago. Peeping over these vast modern erections, too, we may see the fine woods about Holland House, once the favourite residence of the poet Addison, and which, till a very recent period, freely opened its hospitable doors to the leading politicians and distinguished literati of the day, among whom its noble host held himself no mean position; while, in the extreme left, rise the fine timber trees that offer a welcome shade in the gardens of Kensington,—

> " Where elms umbrageous fling their arms around,
> And waxen flowers of chestnut strew the ground;
> Where, half across the sun-illumin'd glade,
> Funereal firs project a black'ning shade;—
> Borne on the breeze, the fragrant scents betray
> The thorn prolific of the luscious May,
> Laburnum pendulous and lilac gay."

In the far distance, too, may be seen the **Surrey Hills** about and beyond Clapham and Wimbledon, that help to form the southern boundary of what geologists call "the London basin;" while immediately adjacent to the Line on the same side, though not visible, owing to a retaining wall, is the common-land, known as *Wormwood* or *Wormholt Scrubs*, an open space of about a hundred and thirty acres, in the parish of Fulham, which is now used as the exercising ground for the household cavalry, and was as much celebrated in the gone-by days of London's pugnacity for the duels of men of fashion, as for the more brutal encounters of men of the fancy. A little further, we pass over the Old Oak Common embankment, whence we get a view of Brentford, Isleworth, and the valley of the Thames; passing nearly at the same time on the north side a curious structure, called the *West*-London Junction

Bridge, which is used not only as a common bridge over the Paddington Canal, but does service, also, as an aqueduct for the canal. Just afterwards, catching a glimpse of Ealing new church, recently built by the munificence of a private lady (Miss Lewis), we arrive at the first stage of our journey,—the

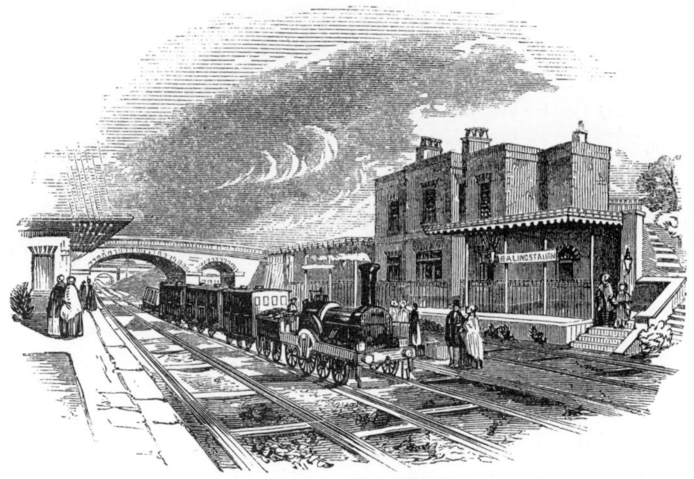

EALING STATION,

five miles and a half from London, which stands on the north side of the Line, opening on the road from Ealing to Twyford. And here let us rest awhile to take a brief survey of the surrounding neighbourhood.

Acton, the first considerable village on the Great Western road, and which lies about a mile south of the Line, enjoyed about a century ago no inconsiderable celebrity as a spa or watering-place; and the near-by hamlets of *Friar's Place* and *East Acton* were filled with persons of all ranks, who came to reside there and drink the saline waters during the summer-months; but, alas! such is the mutability of fashion, that its once-crowded assembly-room has been converted into a private dwelling, and many of its handsomest houses have disappeared. In a political point of view Acton has few associations of interest,—the principal being, that it was the place at which Cromwell, after his victory at Worcester, was met on his return by a congratulatory deputation from the House of Commons and the Corporation of London. The lovers, however, of literature and domestic virtue, will feel a pleasure in being reminded that here for several years resided, on terms of Christian intimacy, the famous Chief Justice, Sir Matthew Hale, and Richard Baxter, the well-known non-conformist Divine. Literature, also, claims to itself another illustrious inhabitant, the misguided, but highly-gifted, Henry Fielding, who resided at *Fordhook House* for some years prior to his departure for Lisbon,—whence, alas! the poor invalid never returned. His parting from his family is thus pathetically described at the opening of his "Journal of the Voyage" thither:—"On this day (Wednesday, June 26, 1754), the most melancholy sun I had ever beheld arose, and found me awake at my house at Fordhook. By the light of this sun I was, in my own opinion, last to behold and take leave of some of those creatures on whom I doated with a mother-like fondness, guided by nature and passion, and uncured and unhardened by the doctrine of that philosophical school, where I had learnt to bear pains and to despise death. In this situation, as I could not conquer nature, I submitted entirely to her; and she made as great a fool of me as she had ever done of any woman whatsoever. Under pretence of giving me leave to enjoy, she drew me in to suffer, the company of my little ones during eight hours; and I doubt not, whether in that time I did not undergo more than in all my distemper. At twelve precisely, my coach was at the door; which was no sooner told me, than I kissed my children round, and went into it with some little resolution. My wife (who behaved more like a heroine and a philosopher, though at the same time the tenderest mother in the world) and my eldest daughter followed me; some friends went with us, and others here took their leave; and I heard my behaviour applauded with many murmurs and praises, to which I well knew I had no title." Poor Fielding died at Lisbon only three months afterwards.

The village of Ealing, originally called *Yelling* or *Yealing,* is a place of no great size, occupying the west-side of a common called by the same name; though, from its position near the fashionable end of London, it has long been a favourite residence, and still comprises within the parochial precincts several handsome seats and villas; among others, *Gunnersbury*, the elegant seat of the Baron de Rothschild, with its choice flower-gardens and beautiful grounds; *Ealing Park*, (the seat of the late Mrs. Lawrence, of Studley Park, near Ripon,) within which is a noble garden, comprising a collection of exotic plants, which, both for their rarity and the tasteful excellence of their arrangement, are not to be surpassed by any other in England; *Ealing Grove, Sutherland House*, &c. &c. About a mile northward, also, is Castlebar Hill, an elevated spot, commanding some pretty views in the valley of the Brent, and downward to its junction with the Thames at Brentford; and here formerly resided General Elliott, Lord Heathfield, the heroic defender of Gibraltar; the late Duke of Kent, the father of our present queen; and Archibald Constable, the once-prosperous publisher of Sir Walter Scott's works, who fell in the same dreadful ruin that involved both printer and author. Ealing old church was rebuilt in the middle of the last century, and is distinguished by that distressing poverty of taste common to the buildings of that era: but its precincts are interesting, as containing the remains, among others, of Serjeant Maynard, a lawyer of great eminence in his day, who was not only retained to impeach the Earl of Strafford and

Archbishop Laud, but was also appointed Protector's Serjeant during the Commonwealth; of Oldmixon, a violent party-writer and dishonest historian, at the beginning of the last century, whom Pope immortalised in his Dunciad;* of the notorious John Horne Tooke, a dangerous demagogue about the time of the first French revolution, and the author of a learned philological work, called oddly enough "The Diversions of Purley;" lastly, of Mrs. Trimmer, a most talented and useful writer of children's books, many of which still enjoy a high reputation.

About a mile and a half beyond Ealing is

HANWELL STATION,

seven and a half miles from Paddington Terminus, which is here raised on an embankment several feet above the natural valley of the Brent,—"Brent, that pretty brook," as Drayton terms it, which flows through the west end of the hamlet under the

WHARNCLIFFE VIADUCT,

a few yards beyond the station. It is 900 feet long, and consists of eight elliptical arches, rising

* Oldmixon was not only a most violent anti-Jacobite, but indulged also in scurrilous abuse of the chief literati of his day, and among others Addison and Pope, the latter of whom has, by way of revenge, given him a distinguished place in his celebrated satire :

"In naked majesty Oldmixon stands,
  And Milo-like surveys his arms and hands,
  Then sighing thus—' And am I now three-score ;—
  Ah, why, ye gods, should two and two make four ?'

He said, and climb'd a stranded lighter's height,
Shot to the black abyss and plung'd downright.
The senior's judgment all the crowd admire,
Who, but to sink the deeper, rose the higher."

about eighteen feet above the natural level; the Line above commanding a fine view on both sides: northward, Hanwell Church, a pretty modern structure, situated close to the Railway; beyond which, the eye embraces a distant view of Greenford and

"Peryvale—prank'd up with wreaths of wheat"—

and beyond that again, to the north-west, of

"That neighbouring hill, where Harrow stands so high;"—

while on the other side the eye looks over green fields towards the village of *Heston*, and then takes a near survey of the

COUNTY LUNATIC ASYLUM,

which with its grounds occupies a space of about eighty acres.

Of external architectural beauty it has, it is true, little to boast; but the whole establishment is in all respects admirably adapted for its purpose, and has accommodation for nearly a thousand patients, besides about a hundred officers and servants. The philanthropist, too, will derive the more pleasure in beholding it, from the reflection, that here has been most fully and successfully carried out a mild system of treatment, which is at once a great source of comfort to the unfortunate inmates, and a high honour to their benevolent and amiable physician, Dr. Conolly, on whom the University of Oxford has lately and very deservedly conferred the highest honorary degree in its gift.

Near the eighth mile-post the Railway crosses the Uxbridge Road, at an angle of about 45 degrees, by an ingeniously contrived timber bridge, well worth the examination of engineers; and, after passing through Southall Park, (the mansion in which, belonging to Lady Ellis, the widow of Sir Wm. Ellis, the late superintendent of the Asylum, may be seen on the north side,) we shall speedily arrive at the

SOUTHALL STATION,

(nine miles from Paddington,) which stands on the north side of the Line, near the road from Hounslow to Hayes,—the former three miles south, the latter about two miles to the north. About Southall itself little need be said, except that it has a cattle market every Thursday, which yields in importance only to Smithfield, and that the Railway Company have constructed, for the convenience of graziers, extensive lairs for the vast quantities of fed cattle brought up weekly by rail from Somersetshire and other grazing districts in the west of England. Those, however, who have leisure for a country ramble, will be repaid for a visit to the curious old Church at *Hayes*, with its carved wood work, circular font, and other architectural quaintnesses; or by a walk southward to the pleasant village of *Norwood*, not far from which is OSTERLEY PARK, a fine demesne of 350 acres, belonging to the Earl of Jersey, who became its possessor through his countess, who inherited it from her mother, the Countess of Westmoreland, the daughter of Robert Child, Esq., the great banker at Temple Bar. The mansion was originally built by Sir Thomas Gresham, the founder of the Royal Exchange, and was frequently visited by our " good Queen Bess." The present house, which is of noble dimensions, presenting a chief front 140 feet in width, with turrets at each end, was erected in 1760, by Sir Francis Child, the elder brother of the person above mentioned.

After leaving Southall, the Railway crosses, within half-a-mile of each other, both the Paddington Canal and the Grand Junction Canal, near the latter of which it runs nearly to the

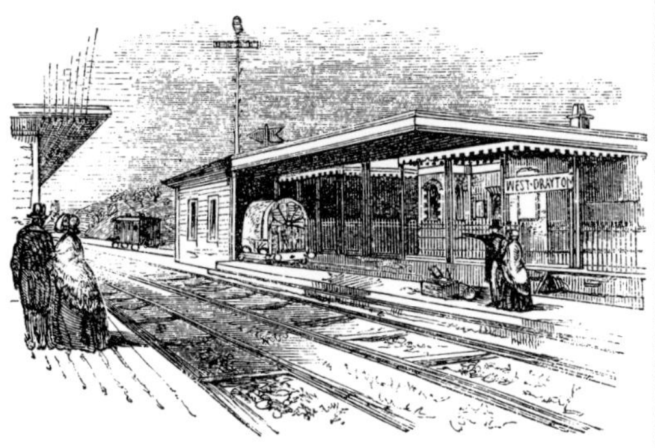

DRAYTON STATION,

thirteen miles from the London Terminus; and near here, on the north more particularly, we may notice extensive brick fields, which furnish a large portion of the supply for the new buildings going on at the north-western end of the metropolis. The rural little village of West Drayton lies almost hidden among fine timber trees, a few yards to the south of the station; and deserves the antiquary's attention both for its interesting old Church, with its ivy-mantled tower, and for its ancient Manor-house, formerly the property of the

Pagets, but for some generations of the De Burghs, a representative of whom is the rector of the parish. Burroughs, the property of Miss Arabin, is also worthy of notice, as having been one of the residences of Oliver Cromwell. The Stag-hounds often meet at Drayton as well as Southall. The angler, too, will find attractions at Drayton, in the neighbouring river Colne; and he cannot do better than seek the humble hostelrie, yclept the Trout, kept by Eastwick, at the hamlet of *Yewsley*, a short half-mile north of the station. He is a civil, obliging fellow; and he rents the fishing of a considerable portion of the river, which here abounds with trout, dace, perch, jack, &c. In the canal, also, there is some very tolerable bottom-fishing. The neighbouring country, too, is pretty and retired, suitable for a ramble; and, if so disposed, the excursionist may have a beautiful walk through *Iver*,* and past Langley Park to the beautiful village of Stoke-Pogis, of which more anon. Hillingdon Church, somewhat more than two miles from Drayton, has a fine cinque-cento monument to Sir Edward Carr, and some monumental brasses, but is otherwise scarcely worth a visit; and about four miles north-west from the station is the market-town of UXBRIDGE (anciently called *Oxbreuge*), on the river Colne, situated, like Drayton, at the extreme western edge of the county of Middlesex. It is interesting to the historian, as having been the scene of the negotiations at the Treaty of Uxbridge between Charles I. and the Parliamentary Commissioners in 1645, and the Treaty-rooms may still be seen at the Crown Inn in a good state of preservation. Two years afterwards the Parliamentary army had its head-quarters here. Uxbridge has, also, been long famous as a market for flour, for grinding which the Colne furnishes abundant waterpower; but the town has lost much of its activity since the removal of stage-coaches by the establishment of the Great Western and North-Western Railways.

Resuming our course along the Railway, we speedily reach the western boundary of Middlesex, formed by the " crystal Colne," and enter Buckinghamshire; nor are there visible from the carriages

* " The church of Iver is one of those old village-structures which is very striking. It has a fine tower, bold projecting buttresses, early Gothic windows, and a beautiful archway leading into the church. Much ivy is growing about it; and the old yew-trees, so frequently to be found in the churchyards of Buckinghamshire, are to be found here. In the church are some curious and interesting monuments and brasses, and one of the oldest fonts I have met with, though sadly disfigured by an unsightly wooden covering. The application of whitewash, also, has been the occasion of concealing many old frescoes in this church."—*Jesse's Favourite Haunts*, p. 152.

any features of remarkable interest, till we enter Slough.   Not far from the

LANGLEY STATION,

however, are two places that may well repay a visit,—*Langley Park*, and *Ritching's Park* and *Lodge*,—the former on the north, the latter on the south side, and about two miles from the station. The manor of Langley came to the crown in the reign of Edward I., and in 1447 was granted to Eton College, but soon after once more reverted to the crown, and was granted in 1564 to Thomas Percy, seventh Earl of Northumberland, who lost it by attainder; and in 1626 it was granted in fee to Sir John Kederminster, of whose family there are several memorials in the church and parish. The estate was purchased in 1738 by Charles, the second Duke of Marlborough, and was purchased from his successor in 1788 by Sir R. Bateson Harvey, Bart., to whose descendants the manor still belongs.

The mansion, however, which is a handsome square building of stone, built by the Duke of Marlborough, belongs to Maurice Swabey, Esq.; and the park around it abounds with fine timber, and commands a good view of Windsor Castle and the forest beyond it.   Ritching's Lodge (now the property of J. G. Murdoch, Esq.) became, in 1704, the property of the first Lord Bathurst, by marriage with the daughter of Sir Peter Apsley; and during his time it was a favourite place of resort for the leading wits of the day:

> " By *Bathurst* planted first, these shades arose;
> *Prior* and *Pope* have sung beneath these boughs;—
> Here *Addison* his moral theme pursued,
> And social *Gay* has cheer'd the solitude."

These lines were added to the writings of Addison, Pope, Congreve, and others, previously cut on a bench in the Park, by the amiable and accomplished Countess of Hertford (afterwards Duchess of Somerset), whose husband purchased the property of Lord Bathurst;—and those who wish for an elegant description of a truly sylvan retreat will do well to peruse the extracts from her ladyship's letters to the Countess of Pomfret, as cited by Mr. Jesse in his " Favourite Haunts," where the present state of the place will be found accurately portrayed, with that happy elegance so peculiar to that earnest lover of nature.   *Ditton Park*, also, at no great distance from Datchet, belonging to Lady Montague, encloses a handsome modern mansion, which is surrounded by a moat, and boasts of some of the finest timber.

Two quickly traversed miles from Langley bring us to the

SLOUGH STATION,

eighteen miles from London, and a most important station, as being the terminus of the WINDSOR-JUNCTION LINE, into which nearly every passing train sends one or more carriages with passengers to Windsor, Eton, and the surrounding neighbourhood: indeed the Windsor traffic, especially during the summer months, and when the Court is resident at the Castle, forms a very important item in the Company's revenues.   The buildings at this station, which are wholly on the south side, are of course made to correspond with the business here transacted; the shed, platforms, offices, and refreshment-rooms, being of suitable size, and admirably arranged to promote the arrival, departure, and general convenience of the many hundreds who daily resort hither, either going to or coming from Windsor. Adjoining the station, also, is a very handsome building, till lately used as an hotel; and most splendidly was it fitted up, when held by Mr. Dotesio; but, as it is soon to be pulled down, it needs no further description. As for Slough itself, though standing in the midst of so many wonders both of nature and art, it contains no feature of any interest, except

THE HOUSE OF THE LATE SIR WILLIAM HERSCHELL,

and the Observatory erected on its top by that illustrious astronomer, whose forty-foot telescope may still be seen encased for better preservation in the garden attached to the mansion. About two miles north-west of Slough, however, is a place equally interesting for its rural beauty and poetic associations,—the village of STOKE-POGIS, where lived and died the poet GRAY, who wrote here (and with reference to this place) his peerless "Elegy in a Country Churchyard." Better words cannot be found to describe this lovely place than those of Mr. Jesse. "Here," says he, "all reminds us of Gray; and his genius seems to make every spot around full of interest. Close to the pretty lodge leading to the church, and in a well-kept and enclosed garden, is a cenotaph erected to the memory of Gray by Mr. Penn of Stoke Park, on which his name is inscribed with some extracts from his poems. From the high bank on which the cenotaph is placed, we look down into one of those deep lanes so full of beauty, and see pretty ferns growing out of the red-sandstone rocks, with violets, strawberries, and other plants inter-

mixed; while, in another direction, and across a

GRAY'S CENOTAPH.

field, is Gray's churchyard, almost surrounded with high fir-trees covered with ivy, which give it a pleasing gloom in summer. This spot it is impossible to approach without feeling that it is one calculated to have inspired the poet with those feelings which drew from him his beautiful and well-known 'Elegy.' Here he wrote—here he wandered—and here he was buried. But where is his monument? We may look for it in vain either in the church or churchyard; and strangers from all parts of Great Britain, and many from different quarters of the world, led hither by their admiration of the poet, return disappointed at finding no record to his memory beyond a simple parish register. Yet how full of interest is the spot we stand on! Here

'Heaves the turf in many a mouldering heap;'—

here are the 'rugged elms'—and here the 'yew-tree's shade;' and there Gray reposes in his 'narrow cell.' Who can be here without feeling his mind softened, and his enthusiasm awakened, especially when he at the same time sees in the distance those spires and towers which crown the 'watery glade' of Eton, and those fields where once the poet says his 'careless childhood strayed.' It is, indeed, almost impossible to doubt that this is the spot where both the Ode and the Elegy were written; for we see the picturesque features of the landscape most accurately placed before us, and almost hear the sounds of rural nature which have been so beautifully and so pleasingly described in those poems." (*Favourite Haunts.*)

The poet's house is still standing, and has been since much enlarged by Mr. Granville Penn, who, till the estate was purchased by the Right Hon. Henry Labouchere, late President of the Board of Trade, owned all the park and adjoining property. In fact, this church and its interesting churchyard may be said to stand within the park, the old manorial house of the Huntingdons and Hattons having formerly been immediately behind them. The estate was purchased by the son of the celebrated William Penn, the founder of the colony of Pennsylvania in the United States; and a portion of the spreading elm-tree, under which he stood when he made the compact with the North American Indians, has been still carefully preserved by the family.

There are other facts, however, connected with Stoke-Pogis that invest it with extreme interest to a lover of history. The manor of this place was brought in marriage to Sir Robert *Pogis*, by a Amicia de *Stoke*, early in the fourteenth century, and their daughter married Sir John Molins, an officer in the court of King Edward III., and who procured a charter at Stoke that his manor should be exempt from authority of King's Marshal. From Sir John Molins this manor descended by marriage to the families of Hungerford and Hastings; of this latter family Henry Hastings rebuilt the manor-house in the reign of Elizabeth, soon after which the estate was seized by the crown for debt. It was granted in fee in 1621, by James I., to the celebrated Sir Edward Coke, who appears to have held it some years before as lessee under the crown: for we find that in 1601, when he was Attorney-General, he gave a sumptuous entertainment to Queen Elizabeth at this place, making a present also to her Majesty, as was the custom in those days, of jewels to the amount of more than a thousand pounds. In 1625, this celebrated lawyer, having lost his favour at court, and been degraded from his high station, was compelled to serve the office of Sheriff for the county, much to the annoyance of his friends, who thought it disgraceful that a former Lord Chief Justice should be compelled to attend on the Judges at the assizes. Sir Edward Coke's eldest daughter married Sir John Villiers, elder brother of the third Duke of Buckingham, who, receiving the reversion of this manor as his dowry, was created a peer in 1613, as Baron Villiers and Viscount Purbeck. This union, however, was far from happy; for Lady Purbeck eloped from her husband in 1621, and lived in adultery with Sir Robert Howard. She was reconciled to her father before his death, and lived with him at Stoke the two years immediately preceding that event, but she afterwards returned to Sir Robert

Howard. In those days, also, these delinquencies were visited with greater severity than in more modern times; for Lady Purbeck was sentenced by the High Commission Court to do penance in a white sheet at the Savoy Church, which she escaped by flight; but the year after her father's death, she and Sir Robert Howard, having before evaded justice, were both taken into custody and committed to different prisons, she to the Gatehouse, and Sir Robert to the Fleet, where he suffered a tedious imprisonment. Lady Purbeck escaped from prison disguised in male apparel, and got over to France. The government demanded her from that court; and whether she was given up, or returned and submitted to her sentence, is not known; but it is certain that some years afterwards she was living in England with Sir Robert Howard in the king's garrison, Oxford, where she died in 1645. In 1647, also, Stoke House was for a short time the residence of the unfortunate King Charles I., when he was a prisoner in the power of the parliamentary army.

We cannot, however, leave all mention of Stoke-Pogis without reference to a favourite resort of the poet Gray, which extends two or three miles to the west of Stoke, called *Burnham Beeches*, well known far and near as a spot of great beauty, singular wildness, and picturesque variety of character; in fact, to any one who has a taste for sylvan scenery, and who can survey, with a painter's eye, the forms presented by single trees, or combined groups of them, it would be difficult to point out a spot more lovely than that now under notice. The Beeches in particular are marvels as bits of forest scenery: "Some of them," says Mr. Jesse, "are of gigantic growth, and of most picturesque character. From their huge trunks, boughs of a size little inferior to the parent stem throw far and wide their horizontal shade, while their no less massive roots, rising above the soil in solid blocks, or twisting their gnarled talons deep into the ground, show at once the firmness with which these vegetable masters are fixed, the power with which they can resist the fury of the storm, and the distance from which they derive that vital nourishment which is seen alike in their strength and beauty, in the tenacity of their fibrous growth, and the splendour of luxuriant foliage." (*Favourite Haunts.*)

"—— Beloved scenes! enough for me
 Through each wild copse and tangled dell to roam,
Amid your forest paths to wander free,
 And find where'er I go a shelt'ring home.
Earth has no gentler voice to man to give,
Than 'Come to Nature's arms, and learn of her to live.'"

Ere finally leaving Slough to pursue our journey westward along the Main Line, let us take a trip along the BRANCH LINE, and

> " Direct our steps to Windsor's stately courts,
>   Explore her halls, her towers, her sacred fane,
>   And treat our eyes with grandeur."

Two short miles conduct us to the Windsor Terminus; and behold us now close under the walls of that Castle, which has been the principal seat of England's monarchs for the last eight centuries, and which still " rears its irregular walls and massive towers, like a mural crown, round the brow of a lofty ridge—waves its royal banner in the clouds, and looks down with a lordly air upon the surrounding world."　To describe England's glory,—

WINDSOR CASTLE,

and its adjoining Park, would require a goodly volume of itself ; and, besides, there are scores of admirably-written descriptions and guide-books that have already done the work far better than we can hope to do it within our limited compass,—and certainly none better than the humble little volume of Edward Jesse, the modern Gilpin. We shall, therefore, merely announce, that the castle on its present site was most probably begun by Henry I., rebuilt and enlarged by Edward III., under the direction of William of Wykeham, who built the round tower and gave the castle nearly the appearance it had at the accession of George IV. St. George's chapel was commenced by Edward IV., and completed by Henry VII., who also added to the castle a pile of buildings in the upper ward, next the royal lodgings.　Henry VIII. rebuilt the great gate of the lower ward ; Elizabeth laid out the celebrated northern terrace, which commands an all but unbounded view over one of the most beautiful valleys of England ; Charles I. also made many improvements, and erected a gate leading to the park ; but the castle was much injured during the civil wars, and the palace of the monarch became his prison.　The whole structure was both enlarged and improved by Charles II., who continued the terrace round the east and south sides of the upper court, and in the reign of his successor the internal decorations and painted ceilings by Verrio were completed.　The succeeding monarchs seldom resided at Windsor, and seem to have cared little about its condition ; nor, much as George III. loved Windsor, as a domestic residence, were any important alterations effected during his long reign ; unless we except some improvements in the Home Park, and the renovation of St. George's Chapel. In fact, the castle owes more of its now splendid appearance to George IV. than to any monarch subsequent to Edward III. ; and " if the latter was fortunate in having William of Wykeham to put *his* plans in execution, George IV. was not less so in having Sir Jeffrey Wyatville to superintend *his* work of renovation."　The castle comprises a lower and an upper ward or court, the first, by far the most spacious of the two, comprising St. George's chapel, the houses for the Military Knights of

Windsor, the Dean's house, Winchester and Salisbury towers, and Henry VIII.'s gateway; while the upper ward, in which the modern improvements have been almost exclusively effected, is formed on the north by the State apartments, on the east and south by the Queen's private apartments and those of the Royal Household; while the west side, which is open, abuts on the Round Tower, the chief entrance into this court being by George IV.'s gateway, at the lower extremity of the Long Walk. Of all the improvements, however, made by Wyatville, by far the most striking was the formation of the Corridor, 520 feet long, which runs round the south and east sides, forming a general communication with the staircases and apartments in the different towers: its ceiling is richly adorned, while on each side through its entire length are bronzes, marbles, busts, remarkable personages, pictures of exquisitely beautiful cabinets, and many other choice specimens of *virtù*, including a peerless collection of paintings by Canaletti. The Grand Staircase, the Guard-room, the Waterloo-chamber, and St. George's-hall, are those of the State apartments that deserve most attention, and especially the last, which for gorgeous splendour, as well as vast size, has not its superior, perhaps not its equal, in any palace in Europe. This Hall, also, has no little interest attached to it, as associated with the Order of the Garter and the Chivalry of England, its flat groined ceiling being decorated with the emblazoned arms of all the Knights of the Order from its first institution to the present time; while on its walls hang the portraits of all the Sovereigns of the Order from James I. to George IV.

Great and glorious, however, as are the historical associations and architectural beauties of the Castle itself, the true lover of nature will seek refreshment for his wearied sight in the spreading lawns, sylvan glades, and shady embowered groves of the wide domain that stretches for several miles to the south and south-west,—

> " Where hills and vales, the woodland and the plain,
>   Where earth and water seem to strive again;
>   Not chaos-like together crush'd and bruis'd,
>   But, as the world, harmoniously confus'd;
>   Where order in variety we see,
>   And where, though all things differ, all agree ;—
>   Where waving groves a chequer'd scene display,
>   And part admit, and part exclude the day;
>   Where, interspers'd in lawns and opening glades,
>   Thin trees arise that shun each other's shades ;
>   Where in full light the russet plains extend,
>   And wrapt in clouds the bluish hills ascend."—POPE.

The northern and eastern terraces, both of them, command magnificent views of the wood and river scenery that extends from the castle walls into the dim far-off horizon; but the most extensive and decidedly the most panoramic view is to be obtained from the round tower; whence, on a clear day, no less than twelve counties can be discerned, including occasionally the Cathedral of St. Paul's in London.

" He who has not seen Windsor Park," says Mr. Jesse, " has not seen the greatest attraction that Windsor possesses;"—for " the vast superiority of Windsor over other palaces, as well as its intrinsic beauty, is bestowed upon it by nature ; and it is in its association with natural beauty, that the greatest pleasure of our visit is derived." In fact, the Park itself will require days for a due inspection of its great and ever-varying attractions ; nor can those be said to have any notion of the real beauties of Windsor, who have been hurried through the usual sights of the castle and then concluded their task with a drive up the Long Walk. Windsor Park, as most persons know, is divided into the *Home* or Little, and the Great Park ;—the former a beautiful expanse of lawn, comprising about 500 acres walled in, and extending round the east and north sides of the castle ; while the Great Park, on the south side, comprehends a much varied, though generally well-wooded surface of about 3,800 acres. The Home Park boasts of some very noble and interesting trees,—especially of an aged oak, generally reputed as

HERNE'S OAK,

the story of which is thus told by Mrs. Page in Shakspere's "Merry Wives of Windsor:"—

"There is an old tale goes, that Herne the hunter,
   Sometime a keeper here in Windsor forest,
   Doth all the winter-time at still midnight
   Walk round about an oak with great ragg'd horns;
   And there he blasts the tree and takes the cattle,
   And makes milch-kine yield blood, and shakes a chain
   In a most hideous and dreadful manner.
   You have heard of such a spirit; and well you know,
   The superstitious, idle-headed eld
   Received, and did deliver to our age
   This tale of Herne the hunter for a truth."
                                        —*Act IV. Scene 4.*

At the south-western corner, too, of the Home Park is *Frogmore*, the seat of her Royal Highness the Duchess of Kent;—adjoining which are the Royal kitchen-gardens, exhibiting as splendid specimens of vegetable and fruit cultivation as are to be found all over Europe. These gardens, which have been formed within the last dozen years, cover a space of about thirty-two acres.

WINDSOR GREAT PARK includes, as its chief object of attraction, the beautiful avenue of trees called the Long Walk, which extends from George the Fourth's gateway nearly three miles in a straight line to an eminence called Snow-hill, the summit of which is crowned by a gigantic, but very mediocre equestrian statue in bronze of the old farmer-king George III.; and the view from its base is probably without its peer in England for luxuriant beauty. "Indeed," says Mr. Jesse, "the spectator hardly knows which to admire most,— the sight of the castle, or the fine trees which surround him in every direction. The beeches in this part of the park are in the highest degree beautiful and picturesque:—herds of deer may sometimes be seen reposing under their shade, while their pendant branches, drooping with an elegance peculiar to this fine forest-tree, seem to invite the traveller to seek for shelter under them; and the fern, the thorn-trees, the masses of wood, the cattle feeding in every direction, all add to the beauty of the scene." The drive, too, by Cumberland-lodge and Bishopsgate to *Virginia-water* is exceedingly beautiful; and, though there are some adjuncts to the scenery of that lake which are not in strict accordance with refined taste, yet the fishing-temple, the lake itself, with the vessels thereon, and a very pretty cottage near its well-planted banks, all produce a very striking effect. Neither must we forget to notice the splendid old timber-trees of the Park, some of which are of enormous size,—especially two near *Cranbourne Lodge*, (about a mile west of Snow-hill,) one of

which, a venerable oak, is thirty-eight feet in girth. The Great Park, however, large as it is, bears no comparison in size with the WINDSOR FOREST of by-gone days, which at one time comprised within its limits considerable portions of Buckinghamshire and West-Surrey, with the whole of south-eastern Berkshire nearly as far as Hungerford, including a territory not less than 120 miles in circuit;—and even so late as the close of the last century the Forest extended over fifteen large manors and nearly 60,000 acres:—but, alas! scarce a vestige of it is left, for, with the exception of some few open tracts adjoining the Park, it has long ago been granted or sold to private individuals, by whom it has been divided, subdivided, and enclosed. Many private residences and estates here,—as Holly Lodge, St. Leonard's Hill, Silwood Park, Sunninghill Park,—deserve, equally with the Park itself, the leisurely examination of such as love the picturesque; but having already dwelt too long on Windsor's wonders, we must content ourselves with a bare mention of their existence on the borders of the Royal demense.

A few words about Windsor itself, on our way back to Eton. It occupies a site partly on low ground south of the river, partly on the slope of the castle-hill, and consists of about half a dozen leading streets, which are respectably built, well-paved, and lighted with gas, besides a handsome suburb towards Clewer;—having also a fine new parish church, a tolerably well-built guildhall, two sets of barracks, &c.; and, with Eton, about 21,000 inhabitants. Its charter was originally granted by Edward, in 1277; and the borough has regularly sent two members to the British parliament since the middle of the fifteenth century. Its members, however, are generally elected at the dictation or under the influence of the authorities at the Castle; to which indeed the town owes all its importance and all its trade. There are several tolerably good inns; and Windsor enjoys a high repute for its excellent ale.

A walk over Windsor-bridge takes us back from Berkshire into Buckinghamshire; and now behold us at ETON, a place full of the most delightful associations, both classical and historical, connecting us more particularly with that period, when our ill-fated monk-monarch, Henry of Lancaster, virtuous, but weak-minded, exerted the better part of his nature in forming an institution that reflects equal credit on its Royal founder, the great William of Wykeham (the originator of the plan), and William Waynflete, its first master and provost.

ETON COLLEGE

was founded by the unfortunate King Henry VI. in 1440, for the support and education of *poor and indigent boys* intended for the church; but though the intention of its royal originator has manifestly been perverted, we can scarcely regret the circumstance, when we recollect that within its time-honoured walls have been educated so many men of whom England is justly proud,—such men as Sir Robert Walpole, Harley, Earl of Oxford, Lord Bolingbroke, the great Earl of Chatham, Boyle the philosopher, the poet Gray, Fox, Canning, Henry Hallam, &c. The present foundation consists of a provost, seven fellows, twelve singing-men and choristers, two schoolmasters (each of whom has six assistants), and seventy boys, now termed "Queen's scholars," who not only receive here gratuitous lodging, board, and instruction, but are afterwards, if found competent, sent to fill the fellowships at King's College, Cambridge. Besides these, moreover, the different masters, as well as certain appointed ladies, called *dames*, receive the stipendiary scholars and boarders (called *oppidans*), who are educated with the others in the college; and among these, averaging about 500, is to be found an abundant sprinkling of the scions of England's highest nobility and landed gentry. The college-buildings are comprised in two quadrangles: first, an outer and very large one, called the *school yard*, in which are the schools, the dormitories, the masters' houses, and a most beautiful chapel (well exhibited in our engraving), of Tudor-architecture; secondly, an inner and smaller one, bounded by the cloisters, and containing the provost's lodge, the fellows' lodgings, the library, hall, &c.; while east of the cloisters are the playing and shooting fields, rich with verdure, and dotted with venerable elms, being bordered southward by the river, of which the boys make abundant use both in bathing and boating. Here may be heard the merry laugh of boisterous youth engaged in various play; here may be seen "hundreds of happy little fellows, as yet by the world unbitted, unharnessed, gambolling over the green, joyous as if care and sorrow were dead," forcibly recalling those lines, in which Eton's gifted son, the poet Gray, has apostrophised with exquisite fidelity the scene of his boyish, careless days :—

> "Ah, happy hills ! ah, pleasing shade !
> Ah, fields beloved in vain ;
> Where once my careless childhood stray'd,
> A stranger yet to pain !
> I feel the gales that from ye blow
> A momentary bliss bestow,
> As waving fresh their gladsome wing,
> My weary soul they seem to soothe,
> And, redolent of joy and youth,
> To breathe a second spring."

The true lover of sylvan, rustic beauty, however, will be scarcely content to quit Etona's "antique tow'rs" without a stroll along the banks of the "silver-winding" Thames, to that favourite resort of anglers, Datchet; where the second Charles, witty but unwise, loved to exercise his skill in fishing, and where Sir Henry Wootton and his fine old friend, good Izaak Walton, enjoyed together the amusement of the rod and line. Neither, if he has leisure to wander further among

> " ———— the sequestered scenes,
> The bow'ry mazes and surrounding greens
> On Thames' banks,"

will he omit to visit Old Windsor, and its cool, retired old churchyard, or the elevated terraces, verdant lawns, and shady walks of " majestic Denham's," Cooper's Hill, or that scene of momentous interest to every free-born and true-spirited Englishman— Runnymede and Charter Island,—

> " Where England's ancient barons, clad in arms,
> And stern with conquest, from their tyrant king
> (Then render'd tame) did challenge and secure
> The charter of its freedom."

The marvels of Windsor have delayed us far longer than we had expected: so, resuming our seat in the train, let us speed onwards towards Reading, the next principal station.

CHAPTER III.

Salt-hill and Eton-montem—Taplow and Maidenhead—Cliefden House—Bray and Ockwells—
Twyford—Henley and Marlow—Sonning-cutting—White-knights—Reading, its Town and
Station—Basingstoke—Newbury—Hungerford.

THE Railway, after it leaves Slough, approaches nearly to the northern boundary of the valley of the Thames, running close at the foot a well-timbered range, rising pretty gently northward, and including the fine woods of *Stoke Park,* and *Farnham-Royal;* the latter of which was long held by the Furnivals and Talbots, as a reward for the feudel service of providing the sovereign with a right-hand glove and supporting his sceptred arm at the coronation. The south side is level, furnishing in some places an open view down to the Thames.

The first object of interest after leaving Slough is *Salt-hill,* the "Mons" of antiquity, whence the long celebrated Eton-festival "Ad Montem," popularly called "Montem," took its name. The mount is supposed to be a British or Saxon barrow; and it seems to have been the custom, ever since the foundation of the college, for the Eton scholars to make a procession every three years, dressed out either in military or fancy-dresses, demanding toll or "salt" of all the carriage-visitors, or other persons of mark and likelihood, whom they might meet in the course of their progress, and—after waving the flag on the top of the mount—concluding the day with festivity. The origin of this custom, notwithstanding much antiquarian research, is not even now satisfactorily known; but it has been supposed to arise from a monkish procession, which took place annually to this mount, and on which occasions consecrated salt was sold to the spectators. Salt-hill, too, deserves notice, as having been one of the most celebrated places in England for the splendour of its posting-inns in the gone-by days of stage-coaches and post-chaises, happily never to return.

The country all around in this part is most beautiful; diversified by country-seats, beechen-woods, numerous orchards, villages, or farm-steads peeping here and there among the trees, and fine, quaint old churches, with their towers, roofs, and walls mantled with ivy; besides which, on the banks of the Thames—the great ornament of this district—are many remains of old monasteries, that brings us back to those times when the threat of "bell, book and candle" spread terror through a priest-ridden country.

Four short miles bring us to the

MAIDENHEAD STATION,

which was the first Terminus of the Line at its opening in June, 1838, and continued so till the July of the following year, when it was opened to Reading. The Railway near this point crosses the Great Western turnpike-road by an oblique brick-bridge and quits the station on a highly elevated embank-

D

ment, extending about a quarter of a mile to the bridge by which the Great Western crosses the Thames, a noble structure of *two* arches, made of brick, dressed with Yorkshire stone, and exhibiting, perhaps, the first example in this country of very flat elliptical arches in masonry, having 130 feet span. If the passenger will cast a hasty glance in passing, he will behold charming river-scenery bounded by woodlands and pleasant fields. A few words, however, must be said about Taplow and Maidenhead; and it is painful to be compelled to brevity, when the beauties are so abundant.

Taplow is the parish on the Buckinghamshire side of

MAIDENHEAD BRIDGE,

(six arches of which, by the way, are in the last mentioned county, and seven in Berkshire;)—and a most beautiful district it is, dotted with pleasant, well-kept villas, intersected with umbrageous up and down lanes, with hedges abounding in wild-flowers;—and then we have, among other lovely places, *Taplow Court*, the seat of the Earl of Orkney, the beauties of which will delight, as often as they are seen. The place we well know ourselves;—but in inviting others to the beautiful spot, we cannot do better than use our old friend Jesse's most pictorial words: " From the abrupt cliffs of Taplow Court you look down upon the beauteous Thames, sometimes foaming over the rugged ledge of a weir, and then pursuing its calm and steady course through rich meadows, or by the sides of overhanging woods and coppices. The corn-mills, with their whitened perturbed waters, the farms and cottages scattered about, the cattle in the meadows, the fishermen in their boats, and the anglers on the banks of the river;—the winding stream itself, and many other objects, produce an effect not easily to be forgotten." Wilson, Gainsborough, or dear old Constable, might have painted a perfect picture from such a description. *Cliefden House*, the seat of the Marquis of Stafford, must be reckoned, however, as the most imposing demesne of the neighbourhood, being placed in a most commanding situation, overlooking all the country southward, possessing a large quantity of fine timber as well as evergreens, and laid out into a variety of walks of all descriptions, commanding fine views, though none equal to that from the terrace, which is a hundred and fifty yards long, and of about the same elevation as the Round Tower at Windsor.

A few words about *Maidenhead* itself,—and we must then onward. The days of its prosperity, as a place of traffic, are past :—time was, when 60 or 80 coaches daily changed here, and innumerable relays of post-horses were required:—nevertheless, though the Railway has taken from the town a very large proportion of that source of income, Maidenhead has vastly benefitted from the influx of persons induced thither by rapidity of communication ; and, perhaps, the town is scarcely worse situated than it was before our iron-roads were conducted thither. It consists of one long street, lined with many genteel residences and good shops, (including two first-rate inns,) forming a pleasant avenue from the bridge, built in 1780, which has thirteen arches, and commands a fine view of the Railway viaduct bridge. It need scarcely be mentioned, that Maidenhead derives its principal importance from the aristocracy of the neighbourhood, to whom it furnishes the principal market. Mr. Garth's hounds hunt the district round,—and perhaps several others :—the river furnishes good trolling, &c. ; and one Jonathan Bond, a civil fellow, who knows all the nooks and corners of the stream, will furnish rods, bait, &c., to those who are strangers to this fine piscatorial district.

We may mention also, that, in the whole valley of the Thames, there is no river-scenery of a calm, sylvan character so beautiful, as that from Maidenhead upwards, past Marlow to Henley :—in fact, the early and late effects of sun-light on the mingled wood and water scenery, especially when autumn has mellowed the sylvan tints, are delicious beyond expression.

Not far from the south side of the Maidenhead station,—for we notice all things as we pass,—is the village and parish of *Bray*, which has acquired a world-wide celebrity from its vicar, one Thomas Brown, who lived in the changeful times of Henry VIII., Edward VI., Mary, and Elizabeth,—and who became three times a Protestant and twice a Papist, in order that he might live and die "vicar of Bray." Probably he had a love for rural retirement, and set that against the turmoils of political agitations:—and were that the case, he was happy in his choice; for more lovely spots than the church and vicarage could scarcely be selected. *Philberds*, the country abode of Nell Gwynn, the best, perhaps, of the second Charles's paramours, is still to be seen within the parish; and the lover of Tudor domestic architecture must make a point of visiting *Ockwells*, not far hence ; which is a perfect *bijou*, in its way, respecting the method of arranging the houses of our gentry in the time of Elizabeth, and which George IV. so much loved that he wished to purchase it for a private residence.

Bysham, on the north side of the Line, was anciently a preceptory of the Knights' Templars;

and in the middle of the fourteenth century an Augustine monastery was founded, the abbey-church of which had once some splendid tombs of the Neville and Montagu families, including the celebrated king-maker, the Earl of Warwick; but these tombs have long been destroyed, and even the site of the church itself is not accurately known. The abbey has been converted into a private residence, the property of A. Vansittart, Esq., M.P. for Reading, and the owner, also, of *Shottisbrooke*, a park three or four miles further, near the south side of the line. It is desirable here, also, to mention, that about five miles north-north-west is *Great Marlow*, a parliamentary borough in Buckinghamshire, on the north side of the Thames, which is crossed here by an iron suspension-bridge;—and it comprises a couple of tolerably well-built streets, with a handsome modern-built church, town-hall, and about 5,000 inhabitants. About a mile and a half north-west is *Stubbings*, and about a mile further, on a commanding elevation, well seen from the Line, is Hall Place, the seat of Sir Edward Clayton East, Bart.

The Great Western, after passing through some pretty long cuttings in the upper chalk beds, at length emerges (30½ miles from Paddington) at

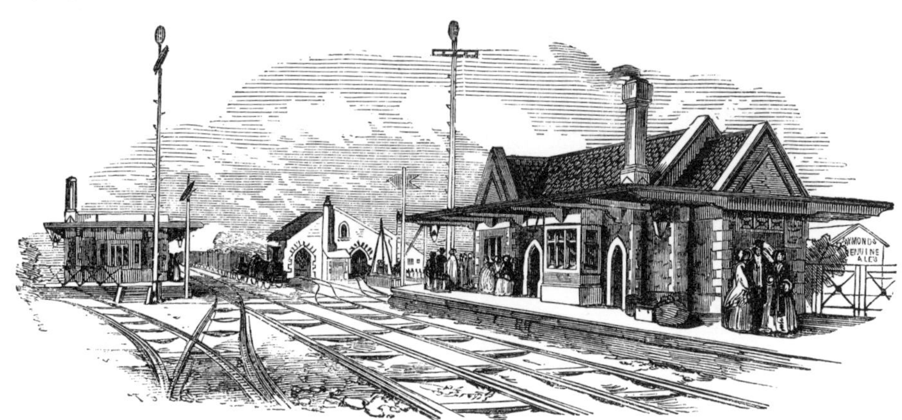

TWYFORD STATION

on the right or east of

"The Loddon slow, with verdant alders crown'd,"

which the Line crosses on a handsome brick viaduct-bridge, spanning a considerable extent of the valley on either side of the divided stream. The station is, like that of Maidenhead, constructed wholly of timber, and near it is a small goods'-shed:—in fact, Twyford is a station of some importance, as being situated in a district that abounds more than most others with fine parks, country-seats, and villas;

besides which it is the station for Great Marlow, Henley, and Wokingham, all of them towns of considerable population.

Near Twyford, close to the village of *Hurst*, is *Stanlake House*, the seat of the Rev. Sir H. Dukenfield, the late highly respected vicar of St. Martin's-in-the-fields ; and three miles northwards is *Shiplake House*, the property of Dr. Phillimore, the celebrated civilian. *Bulmersh Court*, also, and *Woodley Lodge*, both, we believe, belonging to J. Wheble, Esq., lie a little south of the Line, not far from the *Sonning-cutting*. This well-known work is about two miles long, varying in depth from twenty to sixty feet, and having a breadth at the top of about 200 feet in the deepest part:—it penetrates the variegated marls of the plastic clay, and passes almost down to the chalk. The traveller, also, must try to catch a passing glimpse at the two bridges by which it is crossed near its deepest part,—one, rather curious of its kind, made of timber resting on stone abutments, the other of red brick, having three arches, and carrying the turnpike-road from London to Reading. The cutting passed, we are close by *White-knights* on the south side, formerly a seat of the Duke of Marlborough, many years in Chancery, but now the property of the Baron de Goldschmidt:—it was at one time greatly celebrated for its gardens, in which the duke felt great pride; and, we believe, they have been restored to their pristine beauty.

And now behold us crossing the embankment close to the Thames, and leading us to one of the principal stopping-places on the Line,—important also, as being the Terminus of two considerable Branch Lines:—we mean

THE READING STATION.

This is a first-class station, situated in a siding, covered (as will be seen from our engraving) from end to end, and provided with every convenience for the great traffic of so important a place; but still it is by no means so commodious and well-adapted to its purpose as those at Didcot and Swindon.

A few words must be said about READING, of which a good view is gained from the Line, and of which we have given a fair illustration. (*See the opposite page.*)   It is situated precisely where

> "———— clear Kennet overtakes
> His lord, the stately Thames;"

and, indeed, it may most truly be described as situated *on* the Kennet; for its streets are divided by the several branches of that river into numerous small islands connected by bridges. The main streets are spacious and well kept; and there are many handsome brick houses, with several others that present capital specimens of the high gabled architecture of the fifteenth century. Reading has three parish and two district churches; the largest and handsomest of the former being St. Lawrence's, a large structure at the north end of the market-place, having a fine tower of flint and stone, chiefly in the perpendicular style: the other churches are of mixed architecture, and little remarkable, though St. Mary's has a very noble tesselated tower. There are also about a dozen dissenting chapels, including a large meeting-house for the "Society of Friends" (Quakers), who form an important body in Reading. The new county-gaol and house of correction, a castellated red-brick building, with stone dressings, (and which is well seen from the Line before entering the station,) is a very striking specimen of modern-antique architecture, and is internally very well adapted for its painful, but very necessary purposes. By far the most curious feature, however, in Reading, and very interesting to the antiquarian, is the *Forbery*, a beautiful and extensive outwork north-east of the town, now used as a public promenade, and commanding extensive views of the opposite hills in Oxfordshire. It is contained within the space formerly enclosed by the outer walls of the once splendid

ABBEY OF READING,

founded by Henry I., the remains of which prove it to have been both very extensive, and all but impregnable, except to cannon:—it comprised a circuit of about half a mile; the walls of which, made of flint and gravel, and formerly encased in stone, are about eight feet thick. The town, as respects trade, is dependent almost wholly on the wants of a wealthy neighbourhood; but it has, likewise, a few riband and silk looms, some large flour-mills, and pretty extensive breweries.

Reading, moreover, is interesting both to the antiquary and historian, as having been a stronghold of the Saxons before the invasion of the Danes. After the Norman conquest, Henry III. held here one of his earliest parliaments; and several others were held here during the wars of the Roses; besides which, the town became a sort of Oxford for a few years in the thirteenth century, when the students retired during some troubles from that seat of learning. In 1642, the town was garrisoned successively by the two armies of Charles I. and his hostile parliament; and it may be interesting to know that Archbishop Laud, a misguided prelate, (who, by his high church, or rather papistical, obstinacy, was greatly instrumental in the ruin of the unhappy Charles,) was the son of a clothier here, and first saw the light in 1573:—he was a liberal benefactor to Reading, and more especially to the celebrated grammar-school of this place, originally founded in the reign of Henry VII., and afterwards enlarged by Sir Thomas White, the founder of St. John's College, Oxford, who granted them two fellowships in that establishment. Dr. Valpy will long be gratefully remembered by his pupils; among whom are many men of distinction, including that generous friend of literature, Sir J. Talfourd, the author of "Ion."

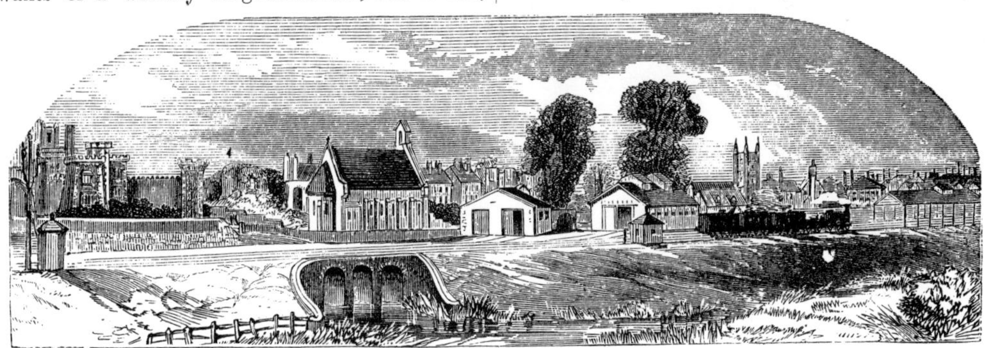

READING FROM THE LINE.

This long description of Reading, however, must not prevent us from doing justice to its environs. Over Caversham bridge, in Oxfordshire, are several beautiful places, near as well as more distant, which amply merit from the sketcher and real lover of scenery very considerable attention; including *Holme Park* (R. Palmer, Esq., M.P.); *Caversham House*; *Mapledurham*, the ancient seat of the Blounts; and *Hardwick House*, the beautiful and well-wooded estate of P. L. Powis, Esq.

Ere we leave Reading, where most of the trains stop to send off living despatches to Basingstoke and Hungerford, and where for the nonce we will suppose our fellow-passenger in a composed, quiescent state, desirous of a little extra information, we shall endeavour to impart to him some small knowledge about the Branch Lines to Basingstoke and Hungerford, for the former of which places Her Majesty took the rail only the other day (August 30, 1851), and passed along the Line by Swindon (where the Royal party partook of luncheon) down to Gloucester when she was compelled to change carriages, and run on the narrow gauge. The Line to Basingstoke passes through a beautiful country, mostly level, and surrounded on each side by parks and estates, including those (at no great distance) of the Iron Duke, his Grace, the venerable proprietor of *Strathfieldsaye*; *Arborfield Hall*, belonging to Sir John Conroy, the intimate friend and trustee of the late Duke of Kent (these two, by the way, the best farmers in the southern part of the county; at least, Caird says so, and he is no mean judge); *Swallowfield Place*, the seat of Sir E. Russell, brother of the talented chairman of the GREAT WESTERN RAILWAY; and *Bearwood Park*, belonging to J. Walter, Esq., M.P., the proprietor of the justly so called "First Journal in Europe," because *it made itself*, and has never since by any talent of the day been surpassed, either here or on the continent.

A few words about Basingstoke, and we must express back to Reading, in order to allow us time to say a few words about Newbury and Basingstoke. It is situated in Hampshire, forty-six miles from the Waterloo Station of the South Western Railway, and rather more than fifteen miles from Reading— on a branch of the Loddon, not far from its source, well-built, and, having a handsome market-house and sessions-court: corn and malt form its chief sources of country business; but the place enjoys some repute, as having given birth to Sir James Lancaster, the navigator (whence Lancaster sound), and Wharton, the historian of poetry. Not far from the town is *Aubrey Camp* (1,000 yards circ), reputed to be a Roman encampment.

A few words now about the NEWBURY AND HUNGERFORD BRANCH LINE. It passes through a beautiful, highly-cultivated country, rising gradually on each side from the valley of the Kennet, near which runs all the way upwards the Kennet and Avon canal, much used before railway times, but now of little service to the country it traverses. *Theale, Aldermaston, Woolhampton, Thatcham*, and *Kintbury* are the intermediate stations that furnish means of communication to the rural districts; but the circumscribed space allowed us will not permit us to enlarge, except on Newbury and Hungerford.

NEWBURY,

of which we here present a sketch, exhibiting the church and the canal before mentioned, is situated seventeen miles west of Reading by railway, and on the great post-road between London and Bath; and it at one time derived its chief prosperity from the posting-business and other resources connected with travelling. Newbury is, also, a large corn-market for the supply both of London and Bristol; and in the town and environs are several flour-mills, malt-houses, and breweries. This town, indeed, as well as Hungerford, is celebrated for its ale; and those who like this beverage will find it here in perfection. Locally considered, this town is oddly laid out; but it has some quaint, gabled buildings, that remind one of the olden days of "Jack of Newbury," one John Winchcombe, a wealthy worsted-weaver of this place, and one of its greatest benefactors. An Inn so called still exists; but the building is modern. Newbury, however, possesses great interest for the historian, inasmuch as two battles were fought here during the civil war between Charles I. and his Parliament,

—the unhappy monarch being present and in command on both occasions. The first was fought on the Wash, September 20, 1643; the second, Oct. 27, in the following year; but neither engagement had any decisive result. The lover of our old true English poetry may here be pleased with a hint, that not far off is *Donnington Castle*, once the property of dear old Chaucer, the earliest and (except Shakspere) the best of our classic poets, who died there in the first year of the 15th century.

HUNGERFORD, the terminus of this branch of the Berks and Hants Line, lies just on the borders, and in the two counties of Berks and Wilts, 26 miles from Reading. It comprises a population of nearly 4,000 persons, and consists of one long street, with a good market-hall; and here, as in Newbury, may be seen a few very good specimens of late mediæval architecture. The breweries of Hungerford are noted; and the water, which furnishes one chief material for its beer, seems to agree capitally with the fish, which of all sorts invite the angler in all directions, both up and down the stream; indeed, trollers and fly-fishers can scarcely choose a better place, unless it be lovely Pangbourne, of which more anon. Hungerford is a very ancient borough, and lays claim to the " Hungerford Horn," supposed to have been given by John of Gaunt with the charter. *Hungerford Park*, the estate of Queen Elizabeth's unhappy favourite, the Earl of Essex, is worth a visit; but the house is modern.

CHAPTER IV.

PANGBOURNE AND ITS RIVER SCENERY—WALLINGFORD ROAD—VALE OF WHITE HORSE AND UFFINGTON—DIDCOT AND ITS STATION—ABINGDON—OXFORD AND ITS BEAUTIES—BLENHEIM—BANBURY.

WE shall now resume our place in the carriage, and hie on to DIDCOT.

On, on—puffing Pegasus, and carry us deftly and with speed on our road:—meanwhile, let us have a pleasant chat with our fellow-passengers, explaining or describing the scenery around, which on the north or Oxfordshire side is unusually beautiful. The reader will see that for himself; but by whatever train he travels—slow, fast, or express, —let him not forget to cast a passing glance at

PANGBOURNE,

(of which we here present a very true and clever sketch, as seen from the Line,) one of those sequestered and lovely spots that would have never acquired more than local fame, had not the Great Western furnished such facilities of approach. It is, indeed, one of those nooks that a lover of sylvan scenery would choose for a long abode; for, while *Sulham*, *Purley Hall*, and *Bassildon Park* exhibit admirable specimens of cultivated scenery,—that on Thames' banks is unequalled in any part of the course of that river; and we speak from ocular knowledge of the whole river from Oxford downwards. Indeed, the words of Byron are truly applicable to this place :—

> " The river calmly swells and flows,
>   The charm of this enchanted ground;
> And all its various turns disclose
>   Some fresher beauty varying round.
> The sweetest heart its wish might bound,
>   On earth delighted here to dwell;
> Nor could on earth a spot be found
>   To nature and to me so dear."

The banks, indeed, are both ways most lovely— quite a treat to an autumn colour-sketcher; and if the angler wants a guide, he will find a handy fellow, one John Chump, who knows and can supply every requisite at marvellously small cost. The church is very old and picturesque—besides which the village has some of those old-fashioned, quaint, gabled houses, that form so striking a feature in the villages and hamlets of our central counties. Our fellow-travellers will at once recognise from this sketch

PANGBOURNE STATION,

one of the prettiest on the Line, and which well harmonises with the scenery around.

Farewell, dear Pangbourne; and now onwards, puff—whistle—and still, once again, puff,—for we are soon to enter on a barren, barely-wooded country, that derives its interest solely from its connection with our national antiquities. The Line crosses the Thames here twice within four miles,—lastly at Moulsford Bridge, which is a very handsome structure of the oolite stone, well worthy of observation, and not far from the spot where the Roman Icknefeld street crosses " beautiful Thames." *Streatly House*, the seat of W. H. Stone, Esq., stands not far hence; and the country—especially the lanes on the Oxford-side—will repay a rambler's visit.

The station next beyond Pangbourne is GORING, which, like the former, is on the estate of *Coombe Lodge*, belonging to S. Gardiner, Esq., an extremely well-wooded property on the north side, which, with the mansion, presents a most beautiful appearance from the Berkshire side of the Thames, which runs for some distance through the grounds. In this district, also, we cross the south-western continuation of the Chiltern Hills, extending over some seventy thousand acres, and composed of chalk both upper and lower, covered at different depths with a clayey loam :—these hills have belonged to the crown from time immemorial, and

have attached to them the sinecure office of " Steward of the Chiltern Hundreds;" by accepting which, any member of the lower house of parliament is enabled to relieve himself of his responsibilities to his constituents. It may be worth while, likewise, to mention the existence of a medicinal spring near Goring, called *Springwell*, which had once a high repute for its curative properties, but which has now fallen into well-deserved discredit.

The next station onward is that of WALLINGFORD ROAD; close to which is the pretty little village of *Cholsey*, and near it Winterbrooke, the seat of Mrs. Kirby. And now we must say a few words about *Wallingford*, three miles north of the Line, one of the oldest and most interesting towns in Berkshire, on the south banks of the Thames, which is here crossed by a stone-bridge 300 yards long, with nineteen arches, and likewise by four drawbridges of quaint, odd-looking construction. The town is well-built and clean, paved and lighted with gas; and it comprises, indeed, for its size, an unusual number of good private residences. It has three parish-churches, all of good architecture; four or five Dissenters' chapels; a free grammar-school; and a respectable town-hall and market-house. No manufacture of any consequence is now carried on : its principal business is that of malting; and, indeed, Wallingford may very truly be described as a neat country-town, respectably inhabited, and a place of no other importance than as the market-town for the surrounding country. It still possesses a fair trade in corn, flour, and hops, being also a parliamentary, as well as municipal borough, sending *one* member to the House of Commons. The neighbourhood abounds with villas and park-residences.

After leaving the Wallingford station we ascend the chalk-marl formation, and now enter on a very different description of country, less wooded, far more open, and in some parts almost wild,— including Lambourn and Marlborough Downs. The whole of West Berkshire to the south of the Line in this part possesses an indelible interest in connection with the struggle between Saxon Alfred and his enemies the Danes. *Blewbury*, in particular, which lies about three miles south of the Line, was the scene of a triumphant victory obtained by our great Saxon monarch over those invaders; and not far off is *Blewburton Hill*, showing the profile of a fine Celtic or Roman entrenchment, closely resembling those to be found near Brightwell and at *Sinodun Hill*, close to the Thames,

> " Where Isis, Cotteswold's heir, long wooed, is lastly won,
> And instantly doth wed with Tame, old Chiltern's son."

The churches in this district, too, comprise many features of peculiar interest to the connoisseur in church-architecture—especially those of *North-Moreton, Brightwell, Sutton-Courtney,* and *Blewbury,* abovementioned.

And now, while we are traversing the country towards Didcot, our fellow-travellers may be somewhat amused with a little, and quite authentic story, about a certain rather eccentric parson, or curate, of Blewbury, (happily some fifty years ago,) the Rev. Morgan Jones, who resided there forty-three years, and whose memory and oddities are still remembered, strongly proving how firm and increasing a hold avarice takes on its victims, when they are once within its grasp. His coats were worn till they required turning; and when torn or rent too much for tacking, he was used to cut pieces off the tail to make good the upper parts, till at length, by repeated cuttings, the unhappy coat in due time became a jacket. One of these extraordinary coats is still, we believe, to be seen within the parish. An odd story, too, is told about the affixing of a shirt-front with a frill to supply the lost tail of his only shirt;—but our lady-readers will say *fie;*—so we will proceed to his diet. He never purchased but three articles,—

two necessaries and one luxury;—the former, bread and bacon—the latter, tea; but of all, the allowance was extraordinarily small: and his beverage was never anything but cold water; except when he could get treated by his friends to good strong ale, which he liked to quaff at others' expense. So likewise with firing; while his parsonage wood-house was crammed with wood and coal, which he could not prevail on himself to use, he would rather roam about the church-yard or fields, or warm his shivering limbs at some poor parishioner's fire, and retire candleless to bed, than use his own stores. Yet this man, who took such pains to make himself miserable, and, through his penury, died worth some thousands of pounds (as may be ascertained at Childs' bank), was not without his good points:—he was a fair scholar, an early riser, very industrious, and a more than mediocre writer of sermons, upwards of a thousand of which were found after his death. He contributed liberally, also, to Bible and Missionary Societies;—and though he often begrudged, and lost a night's rest about the paltry postage of a letter, yet at times pounds would not grieve him. Strange compound!—dreadful lesson on the moral ravages caused by that awful sin of AVARICE; a sin yet more awful when shown in a clergyman, who ought to be his Master's steward and almsgiver!

At length, after a not very interesting ride of about eight miles, we have arrived at DIDCOT, (53 miles from Paddington,) a principal station, and the place of junction for the Oxford, Banbury, and Birmingham Branch;—which, ere we go further, we shall presently describe. As for the village itself, it requires but very little description; for, with the exception of a quaint old church, worth a glance—and that is all,—an ancient

rood or churchyard-cross, here represented, and

a few gabled, pretty cottages, there is nothing worthy of notice.   The village, however, has been

greatly increased since the establishment of a large station here

DIDCOT STATION

is formed on a very large and liberal scale, with every provision for the traffic of an important cross-line, and is covered throughout from end to end.   Spacious as it seems, however, at present, the Company will be compelled to enlarge their premises, when they become connected with the immense additional traffic that will necessarily follow on the opening of a broad-gauge competing-line (so much safer, as well as swifter) with the London and North-Western.

Onward now—leaving for the nonce our friends on the Main-line,—to *cicerone* the visitors of Abingdon, Oxford, Blenheim, &c.   Three miles lead us back to the valley of the Ock, and to Abingdon, just at the junction of that river with the Thames.   The ABINGDON ROAD STATION, about half-a-mile from the town, introduces us to the town itself, which derived all its first importance from its monastery, celebrated from the seventh century, and for some centuries one of the most important mitred abbeys in the kingdom;—of which, at one time, that great old historian, Geoffrey of Monmouth, who lived at the latter part of the fourteenth century, was the honoured lord-abbot.   The town of *Abingdon* is well, though irregularly built, and still presents some of those interesting mediæval bits of architecture, which our modern house-builders either neglect or

despise,—much to their shame.   Abingdon once possessed a thriving cloth trade; but it depends now chiefly on its markets and retail trade,—the sacking-manufacture being of minor importance. It still, however, sends one member to parliament, and is a polling-place for the west division of Berkshire.   There is good fishing both on the Ock and its parent Thames;—besides which, two or three packs of hounds hunt the neighbourhood. *Culham House,* and lovely *Newnham Park,* with its splendid river-scenery, and umbrageous up-hill and down-dale walks, are the chief estates in this vicinity.   *Newnham-Courtney* was frequently visited by George III. and his consort Charlotte; and it is still a sort of show-house, having several good pictures, &c.   The true lover of rustic beauty, however, will give the preference to the pretty village (so carefully provided for by the Countess of Harcourt and his Grace the late Archbishop of York), or to the park itself, and the pretty walks by the river-side, such favourite resorts of the Oxonians during the summer, when "silver Isis" tempts them down her stream.   Here, also, the river furnishes capital fly-fishing.   About three miles north of Newnham is *Cuddesden Palace,* the seat of the Bishop of Oxford, which has been lately much improved by the erection of a chapel in the decorated English style, as well as other additions in equally good taste.

OXFORD STATION.

Look thither, as we go forward, fellow-traveller; —see you no object of interest in prospect? Do you not, when approaching Oxford,

> "In tow'ry dimness, gothic, vast, and grand,
> Behold her palaces of learning stand?"

OXFORD is, without doubt, greater as an University than either Padua or Paris;—great, in early days, because she was the all-but exclusive protectress of all the learning in England,—great in the middle ages, because she struggled to support the doctrines of the Reformation,—great in later days, because she has given a sound and elegant education to the men on whom the destinies of this empire have chiefly depended. In fact, no place has exercised hitherto such an influence as Oxford on the interests of this country :— God grant that this power may never hereafter be ill-exercised.

The city stands on a plain, in the midst of meadows thickly planted with trees, surrounded on three sides by the Isis, and its northern contributary, the Cherwell : and it has an imposing external appearance from whatever side it may be viewed ; but more especially from the adjacent high ground on the London and Abingdon roads.

The *High Street* is one of the finest in England ; not only for its width and regular arrangement, but for the beauty and magnificence of the churches and collegiate edifices lining it on both sides. The towers of Magdalen and All Souls' Colleges, (especially that of the former, which, from its lightness and the beauty of its proportions, is one of the finest features in Oxford,) the noble fronts of University and Queen's Colleges, and St. Mary's, the University Church, are its chief and most admired features. Three other streets meet it at its west end ; one of which, called the *Corn-Market*, leads northward to the airy suburb of St. Giles's ; while the second passes southward by the town-hall, and the noble building of Christ Church, towards Abingdon ; a third, called *Queen Street*, running westward in continuation of High Street, past the old castle, (now the gaol,) into the low and densely peopled parishes of St. Ebbe and St. Thomas. Parallel to and north of High Street, is another fine, though not long line, called *Broad Street*, in which are Balliol, Trinity, and Exeter Colleges, the Ashmolean Museum, Clarendon Rooms, Sheldonian Theatre, &c.; and between High Street and Broad Street is an oblong space, occupied by a quadrangular building, forming a hollow square, round which are the academical "Schools," the upper stories being occupied by the Bodleian Library and Picture Gallery. The schools used once to be employed as places for disputations ; but they are now the examination-halls for proving the abilities of candidates for degrees ; and many a stout heart has faltered at entering the dark gateways that lead to these chambers of torture and trial !

Between the schools and St. Mary's Church, flanked east and west by All-Souls' and Brasenose Colleges, is the *Radcliffe Library*, a circular Grecian edifice, surmounted by a dome, and contrasting rather strangely with the Gothic structures by which it is surrounded ; but the interior contains an interesting library, &c.; and its external gallery commands a most splendid view of the entire city and its surrounding neighbourhood :

> " Spire, tow'r and steeple, roofs and radiant tile,
> The costly temple and collegiate pile,
> In sumptuous mass of mingled form and hue,
> Await the wonder of th' unsated view."

St. Giles's and Beaumont Streets, on the north side of the city, are lined with substantial private dwellings ; besides which, St. John's and Worcester Colleges, and the *Taylor Building*, a large modern structure of Corinthian architecture, (used for the purpose of instruction to the students in the modern languages,) greatly contribute to the embellishment of this part of Oxford. This latter structure, as being a more modern erection, indicating fresh vigour in the time-honoured nursing mother of our church, we shall describe more at length. It was built from designs by C. R. Cockerell, R.A., and the beauty of detail in very many parts of the building deserves the highest praise. The Taylor Institution occupies the east wing, facing St. Giles's, being entered from that street through columns, on whose capitals are four statues representing European languages. Within is a handsome, lofty library, 40 feet square, with lecture-rooms, &c. The galleries, facing Beaumont Street, comprise on the ground-floor a sculpture-gallery (180 feet by 28), with an additional wing (90 feet by 28) ; and on the first floor a fire-proof gallery (70 feet by 28), with a picture-gallery (100 feet long, 28 wide, and 28 high) ; besides which, there is also a basement story, with lodgings for the keeper. In the west wing of the ground-floor are placed a portion of the original casts of the late Sir F. Chantrey's leading works ; and the gallery upstairs contains the celebrated collection of original drawings, one hundred and ninety in number, by M. Angelo and Raffaelle, purchased partly by subscriptions in the University, but chiefly by the noble donation of five thousand pounds by the late Earl of Eldon.

Here, also, we may mention, that in the northern suburb of Oxford are two important buildings, which, owing to their distance from the denser part of the city, are sometimes overlooked by visitors,—the *Radcliffe Observatory*, and the *New Clarendon Printing Office*. The former is a lofty octagonal building enclosed within prettily-arranged grounds, and well-provided with all the complicated and costly apparatus necessary for celestial observations. The latter is a most spacious and elegant structure, consisting of a centre and two wings running backwards ; and it is within this edifice that all the Oxford Bibles and Prayer-books, as

well as all the works produced by the University, are printed, under the direction of a supreme managing committee, called the " Syndicates of the Press." The whole is worked by steam-power ; and so perfect is the establishment in all its parts that it amply deserves a lengthened visit.

St. Mary Magdalene, at the junction of the Corn-Market with Broad Street, is in the decorated style ; but for its own merits scarcely deserves a separate notice. What renders it chiefly interesting is the addition of a large aisle to the church, and the erection to the north of the churchyard of a very handsome Gothic structure, (for a sketch of which we are indebted to Mr. J. H. Parker, the enterprising publisher to the University,) more commonly called

THE MARTYRS' MONUMENT,

erected by subscription, in commemoration of the martyrs, Cranmer, Latimer, and Ridley. It was constructed on the model of Queen Eleanor's cross at Waltham, has a total height of 73 feet, is divided into three stories, and is ornamented with statues, by Weekes, of the three martyr-prelates.

Carfax, or St. Martin's, the corporation-church, facing the west end of High Street, is an oblong stone building, with a low tower. *All Saints*, in the High Street, is in the Grecian style : the roof is entirely supported on the side walls, and the whole is surmounted by a tower and spire.

OXFORD FROM THE MEADOWS, NEAR THE RAILWAY STATION.

The *Cathedral Church* connected with Christ-Church College, presents the styles of different ages, from the 12th to the 16th century: it is built in the form of a cross, and measures, from east to west, 154 feet; the length of the transepts being 102 feet, and the height from the floor to the roof, 42 feet. At the intersection of the nave and transepts rises a tower, surmounted by a spire 146 feet in height. The carvings of the choir are very elaborate, though somewhat heavy; and in some of the windows are fine specimens of painted glass; besides which, there are some fine tombs and statues. Unfortunately this cathedral church is so hemmed in by college buildings and gardens, that no view of the whole can be well obtained.

St. Mary's Church (used by the University for the academical sermons, Bampton lectures, &c.) is a fine structure, in the perpendicular style, surmounted by an elaborately ornamented tower and spire, 180 feet high. The side towards the High Street, however, is disfigured by an incongruous porch with twisted columns. A visit to this church during the University sermon, morning or afternoon, will be found amply to repay the trouble; for there may then be seen dressed in their suitable academical dresses all the members of the University, from the vice-chancellor and the proctors to the lowest under-graduate.

St. Peter's-in-the-East, near Queen's College, the oldest church in Oxford; its original portions are Norman, but it has had many introductions and alterations, mostly in the perpendicular style, which have greatly altered its exterior appearance. Its curious crypt, however, is quite worthy of a close examination; for it is one of the best extant.

The other churches of Oxford deserve no particular description. The Roman Catholics have a small chapel in the eastern suburb; and there are places of worship for Wesleyan and Calvinist Methodists, Independents, and Baptists. Oxford has also a handsome town-hall, music-hall, good covered market-place, new sessions-house, county-gaol, two or three banks, and several first-rate inns.

The great glory of Oxford, however, after all, consists in its buildings devoted to collegiate education, which far surpasses those of Cambridge in number, and in extent and beauty. Most of them are built in the style peculiar to the 15th and 16th centuries; but a few more modern erections, as Queen's and Worcester Colleges, with Peckwater in Christ-Church and the Park Buildings of Magdalen Colleges, partake more of the Grecian style, introduced in the 17th century. The colleges are chiefly built in hollow squares, round which are the members' rooms; and the Quadrangles of Christ-Church, All Souls, Magdalen, New, and Brasenose Colleges, are very large and imposing. The chapels, halls, libraries, and gardens of these establishments are likewise extremely beautiful.

As, however, there are so many objects to admire, a mere excursionist may require a few hints.

Christ-Church, with its splendid timber-roofed hall hung with pictures, and the beautiful staircase leading thereto; *Magdalen; All-Souls,* with its fine library; and the *Schools,* with the Bodleian library and picture-gallery, are the first objects; —nor should he forget to visit the *Christ-Church Meadows* and *Magdalen Walks,* which are of great extent and beauty,—the former remarkable for their cheerfulness and animation, from the throng of gownsmen that frequent the river at the southern extremity,—the latter for their sylvan solitariness and classic retirement.

We shall now present our readers with a list of the colleges and halls of this seat of learning, the dates of their foundation, and the number of members in 1852 :—

Colleges and Halls.	Date of Foundation.	Members in 1852.	
		M.A.	Total.
University	1249	137	264
Balliol	1268 ?	188	347
Merton	1264	95	175
Exeter	1314	247	453
Oriel	1326	198	387
Queen's . . .	1340	153	264
New	1386	98	183
Lincoln	1427	124	222
All Souls	1437	84	117
Magdalen	1456	148	188
Brasenose	1509	259	411
Corpus Christi . . .	1516	103	137
Christ-Church . . .	1525 & 1532	423	729
Trinity	1554	157	289
St. John's . . . -	1555	190	343
Jesus	1571	76	152
Wadham	1613	164	314
Pembroke . . .	1624	97	217
Worcester . . .	1714	173	323
St. Mary Hall . . .	1333	34	118
Magdalen Hall . . .	487	118	263
New Inn Hall . . .	1392	18	66
St. Alban Hall . . .	1547	7	22
St. Edmund Hall . . .	1269 & 1559	59	96
19 Colleges, 5 Halls .	. .	3,352	6,080

The buildings belonging to all or most of these societies, are of great extent and beauty, comprising several quadrangles, and laying claim to considerable architectural elegance. The libraries and dining-halls are on a large scale, and the rooms within the colleges are capable of accommodating from a hundred to five hundred students, according to their size, and the number of their members. Oxford, indeed, from the great number of its fine academic buildings, has a very imposing appearance when seen either near or at a distance;

and it has been not inappropriately called a city of palaces, vying in external and internal beauty with the finest cities.

Some of our graver readers, however, may desire to know something more than the buildings can tell them of the education pursued within these time-honoured walls. This is not the place to discuss such subjects; but it may be well to mention that the attainments of a graduate *must* be those of a thoroughly-trained Christian gentleman, and, *where distinction is aimed at,* reach a high degree of science and erudition. The term of residence averages about three years, and the *necessary* expenses during the time amount to about £500 or £600, according to the college at which the student enters.

Our sketch of Oxford has been necessarily very brief and circumscribed; but those who wish more information may use with confidence the capital " Visitors' Guide to Oxford," which is accurate as well as full. It is published by J. H. Parker, and contains numerous beautiful illustrations. One word more ere we leave :—the month of June is by far the best in the year for visiting this seat of learning; inasmuch as the junior members about this time assume, as it were, the butterfly state, and attend far more to Bullingdon cricket-ground, boating on the Isis, country excursions, &c.; any thing, in short, but the classic lore, which calls Alma Mater's children to these academic haunts. The boat-races are especially worthy of a visit; and one of them generally takes place an evening or two before " Commemoration," the great festival of this ancient, hallowed, seat of learning.

Farewell, classic Oxford, scene of pleasant recollections and happy hours to more than half the aristocracy and clergy of England—scene of gaiety and trial too ;—and now let us onward to another favourite resort of the Oxonians—BLENHEIM, the ancient Woodstock Park, which erewhile bore silent witness to the loves and troubles of Henry III., and his unhappy mistress, the fair Rosamond, but which has since gained a world-wide celebrity, as having been the gift of the English nation to the great John, Duke of Marlborough, our triumphant defender during the thirty years' war in Germany, where he earned many brilliant victories. The grounds are beautiful, the timber on the estate is unsurpassed; but Sir J. Vanburgh's production in the shape of a palatial residence can really please no one of correct taste, though its parts possess many good features. The old lines about it are too hackneyed for repetition. It is of great extent, comprising a frontage of about 350 feet; and from

VIEW OF BLENHEIM FROM THE LAKE.

a distance has a very imposing effect. The interior, however, is far more to our taste:—the hall is magnificent, still adorned, we believe, with the trophies of the great predecessor of the " Iron Duke," and having a fine painted ceiling. The state-rooms, too, are splendidly furnished with Gobelin's tapestry, and pictures by all the choicest masters of the great schools of art, with several *chefs d'œuvre* by Sir J. Reynolds. In a separate wing, also, are some very fine, but not over-delicate, pictures, said to be by Titian, that are well worthy of a visit from the lover of art. Indeed, Professor Waagen, who is deemed by all to be an excellent judge in all matters of taste, says respecting Blenheim, that "if nothing was to be seen in England but this seat, with its park and rich treasures of art, there would be no reason to regret the cause of a journey to this country." The state bed-room, too, though now rather tawdry through decay, must at one time have been very splendid; —but, after all, the chief attraction to a man of real taste and education is the splendid library, about 200 feet long, which, independently of being a very handsome apartment, possesses a valuable collection of works belonging to a former day; but neither this, nor, indeed, any part of the property has been much improved either by the present duke* or his father, the former owner of

White-Knights, near Reading;—to whom, however, Blenheim is indebted for its fine gardens running level with the basement-story. The grounds throughout are worthy of a lengthened examination, and many spots may be found in the glades of the park, that will amply repay an artist's visit.

When dilating on Blenheim, however, we must not forget to make fitting mention of the ancient borough of *Woodstock*. It is situated on the Glyme, a stream which supplies the magnificent sheet of water in Blenheim Park, and is an extremely clean, open, and well-built country-town, though, withal, very dull and inanimate, owing, it

* A few very pertinent observations about the state of West Oxfordshire, and particularly on the estates of his Grace of Marlborough, have been made by one of the best agriculturists in Great Britain; and we feel great confidence in quoting them. "The country exhibits a poverty-stricken and neglected look. The largest estate in West Oxfordshire, is that of the *Duke of Marlborough at Blenheim;*—many farms on which have from various causes fallen under the Duke's own manage-

ment, so that he now farms himself upwards of 5,000 acres of his own land. This is partly to be ascribed to the general raising of rents, unaccompanied by improvements of the land or increased stock-accommodation; and the result has been, that as soon as a farm is so completely reduced as to be untenable, it reverts to his Grace. The country exhibits a poverty-stricken and neglected look; and there is no confidence of a friendly or even feudal character between landlord and tenant. This is much to be regretted; as the farms are many of them very desirable in point of extent and quality, varying from 600 to 900 acres, and well adapted for green crop and stock-farming. The average produce of wheat for several miles round Woodstock is stated at twenty bushels, and barley at forty bushels per acre:—turnips are a light, poor crop. Few sheep or cattle are kept; and stock-feeding meets with no attention. Wages range between 9s. and 11s. a-week. As to the houses of the Oxfordshire farmers, neatness and order characterise them internally; and their fronts are generally so arranged as to command an agreeable prospect. They are usually so placed as to be in proximity to, and in full view of the farm-yard; so that every thing that goes on there may be under the immediate eye of the owner; and each farm-house has attached to it a good sized vegetable garden, and not unfrequently a piece of well-stocked orchard ground. The landlords, as a body, take little interest in agriculture, few being practically acquainted with farming; besides which, the agents whom they appoint are as little qualified to judge as themselves, being mostly lawyers."—*Caird's Eng. Agric.* pp. 24—28.

is supposed, to the decline of the coaching and posting-business consequent on the opening of the Banbury Branch of the Great Western. The church is a handsome structure, partially reconstructed in 1785, when a tower was added to its western end. There is also a town-hall, where the petty-sessions and debt-court are held; under which is the market-place. Woodstock at some former period had a thriving manufacture of polished steel-articles, much prized for their delicate workmanship; but this branch of industry is now wholly extinct. The manufacture of doe-skin gloves, also, introduced at a much later date, even in 1,200 hands, chiefly women and girls, has greatly declined, principally owing to the substitution of thread and cotton for leather-gloves, and the general disuse of wash-leather gloves in particular; the result of which, combined with the impoverished condition of the Marlborough family, has led to a decline both in the prosperity and population of Woodstock. The borough sent two members to the legislature from the 13th year of Elizabeth down to the Reform Act, which, while enlarging its electoral boundaries, deprived it of one of its members:—that remaining is still substantially the nominee of the Duke of Marlborough. All traces of old Woodstock Palace, which stood on the north side of the Glyme, have long disappeared; but it will ever hold a bright place in history, as having been the birth-place of Edward the Black Prince, the illustrious son of an equally illustrious sire, Edward III.; and it was subsequently inhabited by various monarchs, down even to the times of the first Stuarts. Tradition, also, assigns Woodstock as the birth-place (A.D. 1328) of GEOFFREY CHAUCER, the great father of English poetry; and the house where he lived is still shown.

At length we have arrived at BANBURY STATION, the present terminus of the Oxford and Birmingham Junction-line; and we have here reached, indeed, the land of cakes for the south, from which it derives a sort of world-wide celebrity,—and justly so, for Banbury—real Banbury cakes, are exceedingly good eating. The town of Banbury, however, has other and more solid claims on our attention than cakes; for it enjoys a very extensive retail and carrying trade, and has also numerous fairs and large weekly markets, together with some manufactures of saddlery, &c.; and the neighbourhood is celebrated for its excellent cheese. Banbury, which stands not far from the source of the Cherwell, an affluent of the Thames, is clean and fairly built, but has no architectural features worthy of remark, except perhaps its church, which is an imitation of St. Paul's in London,—and, like all mere imitations, a failure. There is also a very fine Gothic chapel for the Roman Catholics;—and there are several places of worship for different classes of Dissenters. This place is a corporate town, also, and under the Reform Act sends one member to the House of Commons. Its ancient Saxon name seems to have been *Banesbrig*; and from the number of Roman coins and various other antiquities of the same era that have been discovered here, it has been thought by some antiquarians to have been a Roman station. It was afterwards the residence of the then powerful bishops of Lincoln, who erected a castle here in the twelfth century, which was occupied as an episcopal residence even after the Reformation:—some ruins of it may still be seen. A battle was fought at Edgecote, about three miles hence, during the wars of the Roses (1469), between the Earls of Warwick and Pembroke, ending in the defeat and death of the latter, as well as the capture of Edward IV. a few days subsequently. In the parliamentary wars the inhabitants took part with the Puritans, and were twice besieged by the Royal army. In the neighbourhood of Banbury are *Wroxton Abbey*, belonging to Colonel and the Baroness North; *Brighton Castle*, the estate of the Rev. Lord Say and Sele; and *Wykham Park*, the property of Mrs. Stuart.

In a future edition, the continuation onward to Birmingham will be given, with illustrations and all particulars of the intermediate scenery, and places of note; nor do we entertain the slightest doubt, that, when the Line is opened thus far, the great mass of the best passenger-traffic from Birmingham to London will pass over the broad-gauge railway. Time will show.

The following is a list of the stations from Banbury to Birmingham, with their distances from Paddington:—

	Miles from Paddington.
Copredy	89½
Fenny Compton	94¾
Harbury	100
Leamington	106
Warwick	108
Hatton	111½
Kingswood	116
Knowle	118½
Solihull	122¼
Acock's Green	124½
Birmingham	128½

CHAPTER V.

WANTAGE AND ALFRED THE GREAT—FARRINGDON—PUSEY AND ITS MODEL-FARM—COLESHILL PARK—
UFFINGTON AND THE WHITE HORSE—LECHLADE—SWINDON, ITS STATION AND DEPÔT—WOOTTON-
BASSETT—AVEBURY AND ITS DRUID TEMPLE—MALMESBURY—CHIPPENHAM—MELKSHAM TROW-
BRIDGE—BRADFORD—FROME—BOX-HILL AND ITS TUNNEL—BATHFORD—APPROACH TO BATH.

HAVING thus given an account of the Oxford and Birmingham Branch-line, as far as it is now open (September 15, 1852), we shall once more resume our journey to Bristol, and, with one small exception, shall pursue it uninterruptedly, till we arrive at that "royal and free city." A run of rather more than three miles brings us to STEVENTON STATION, (56¼ miles from Paddington,) a small intermediate station in a bare and thinly populated country, having no feature of interest near it; unless, perhaps, we except *Milton* and *Milton-house*, the property of John B. Barrett, Esq., about a mile to the north-east. Our next stage takes us to the WANTAGE ROAD STATION, which, though only intermediate, is far from unimportant, as being the point of connection with the ancient royal town of Wantage, (two miles south,) which had the honour of giving birth to our true English-hearted and most learned monarch, Alfred the Great, who first saw the light here, October 25, A.D. 849. Wantage, however, has other claims on attention besides its antiquity; for it stands on the Wilts and Berks canal, and at the junction of two great turnpike-roads—one from Hungerford to Oxford, the other from Farringdon to Wallingford; besides which, it has a rather extensive trade in fine sample corn, and also in malt and flour; and it boasts also of some manufactures of coarse cloths, sacking, and cordage. The church, which is cross-shaped, is really very handsome, and worth a visit; and it has a fine embattled tower. The parish extends over about 7,500 acres; and comprises about 5,000 inhabitants. The surrounding country was formerly the patrimony of the Anglo-Saxon monarchs, and the whole district is to this day rich with monuments of the sturdy Saxon race.

Four short miles further take us to FARRINGDON ROAD STATION, six miles south-east of the town of that name, from its proximity to which it derives its principal importance. *Farringdon* lies at the western declivity of a hill, on which stands the church, an old and extensive cruciform building, which is well worth a visit, as containing some curious old monastic carvings, and several fine monuments. Above the church, also, is a pretty grove, which, from its elevation above the surrounding country, commands pretty extensive views over the three counties of Oxford, Gloucester, and Wilts. The town itself is respectably built, and very clean, showing in its houses many remains of that gabled architecture, so common throughout the southern counties of England: it has a good town-hall, some valuable charities, and is one of the polling-places for the county of Wilts. The parish extends over about 7,000 acres, and comprises about 4,500 inhabitants.

Neither are we now more than four miles distant from an estate of no small note among scientific agriculturists—*Pusey*, belonging to Philip Pusey, Esq., a visit to which will, no doubt, be interesting to those who are fond of rural pursuits. Nearer at hand, also, is *Buckland*, the ancient manor of the Throckmortons, the mansion of which was rebuilt in the middle of the last century, under the superintendence of the elder Wood, of Bath. The pleasure grounds are laid out with great taste, and command some fine views.

Shortly after passing the seventy-first mile-post, we arrive at the SHRIVENHAM STATION, on the extreme western border of Berkshire, a very small intermediate station close to a village of that name, having an interesting Gothic church. From this part of the Line may be seen to the north-east the fine woods of *Beckett Park*, belonging to Viscount Barrington; the house is modern, and in excellent taste. About five miles further, also, in nearly the same direction, is *Coleshill Park*, the noble seat of the Earl of Radnor. The mansion was built from the designs of Inigo Jones in the middle of the seventeenth century, and is generally recognised as one of the best extant specimens of his style. Its plan is that of a perfect square, comprising a basement and two principal stories, with a high sloping roof, the whole crowned by a balustrade. The grounds are extremely beautiful, presenting in every direction that pleasing variety of hill and valley, which gives so fine an effect to the beauties of well-wooded park-scenery.

Turn we now southward, and we may see on the steep escarpment of yonder eminence, called *Uffington Hill*, a rude figure, known all over the country, of a *White Horse* in a galloping posture, formed by making trenches to lay bare the chalk beneath the scanty herbage. The figure is 380 feet long, and covers about an acre of ground, not a sixth part of which, however, is white. Tradition declares it to have been carved as a memorial commemorative of a victory gained over the Danes by Alfred and the West Saxons in the year 871. The lover of British antiquities will here not forget to visit *Wayland Smith's Cave*, which is well described in Sir Walter Scott's "Kenilworth." It seems to be the combination of a cromlech with a regular druidical circle, the remains of which may still be traced. The cave is formed by three stones set on edge, so as to form a chamber with a fourth to serve a roof. There are traces also of a cross-shaped alley or avenue, open at one end leading to the cromlech. The whole neighbourhood, however, abounds throughout with British antiquities.

It may be well here to mention, that two miles west is *Lechlade*, a small but well-built town, or rather village, of Gloucestershire, at the confluence of the Lech with the Isis, having a fine ornamented English church with a lofty tower and spire, with some 1,500 inhabitants. And now we will away to Swindon, indulging by the way in a short gossip about the rural culture of the country about the Vale of White Horse. The population, as might be expected, is almost exclusively agricultural, employed in cultivating the arable district in the lower part of the vale, which, except a few low pasture meadows, is wholly laid out in crops. The upper part of this beautiful valley is used pretty generally as pasture-land; and the chalk downs, with a few slight exceptions, are employed as sheep-walks.

The scream of the whistle, the scraping sound of the brakes, and a sensible diminution of speed, at length give a sort of brief intimation that we are approaching an important stage or resting-place on our journey. Swindon, all-important Swindon; who that knows aught of railways, or railway travelling, has not heard of Swindon's world-wide reputation, as well for the vastness of its workshops and engine depôt, as for the admirable and splendid accommodation that it furnishes to the way-worn traveller?

THE SWINDON STATION,

which we are now entering, is of vast size, about 184 feet from east to west, and rather more in breadth between the enclosing walls, covered in from end to end, and provided on either side with ample platforms, (each 14 feet wide,) on which passengers may alight and promenade,—if they please, or have no more pleasing occupation in view,—till the train is ready to start with a fresh engine. For ourselves, however, pleading a weakness towards banbury-cakes and sherry-cobler, we shall bend our steps towards the refreshment-rooms, whose folding doors, and snug interior, tempt the passenger to while the few fleeting minutes allowed him, in procuring the services of the pretty and obliging Hebes that preside at the elegant and well provided counters, under the superintendence of that paragon of caterers, Mr. Phillips.

FIRST-CLASS REFRESHMENT ROOM, SWINDON.

These rooms (for there is another on the up-platform, which is its exact counterpart,) are of most noble dimensions, having their walls and ceiling elaborately decorated in arabesque, and supported by columns, most exquisitely painted in imitation of inlaid woods;—nor would the mirrors, hangings, and furniture that adorn them, do shame in comfort and elegance to the dining-rooms of our first nobility,—especially on that side of the counters which is set apart for first-class passengers. It need scarcely be added, that every article of food, from a banbury-cake or a sandwich, to a basin of turtle or a cold fowl,—every assuager of thirst, from humble tea or bottled stout, to iced-lemonades or aristocratic champagne, is provided with a kind of *heigh-presto* rapidity, that might almost vie with the high railway speed, for which this great Line has long and justly been celebrated. But whence come, and how are prepared, all these viands and choice refections to tempt our readers' appetites? A glance down yonder staircase will solve the riddle; for it leads to kitchens below us, amply fitted with culinary apparatus, pantries, and store-rooms filled to repletion with every solid article of food that reasonable men can wish for, and spacious cellars, whose bins are full of the choicest wines, and whose shelves groan under the weight of hundreds of dozens of porter, ale, soda water, &c. Once more, look up yonder wide and splendid staircase, and, if you have time, ascend to the upper floor:—there you will find a noble coffee-room, private sitting-rooms, &c., (with bed-rooms on the other side of the Line,)—in fact, all the appurtenances of a first-rate family hotel, nearly every window of which commands magnificent views of the Wiltshire and Berkshire scenery for many miles round;—and should any of our gentlemen fellow-passengers desire the luxury of the fragrant cigar, which either on the platforms or in the carriages is

"Bann'd and barr'd, forbidden fare,"

he may indulge therein to his heart's content in the cheerful covered gallery which runs above and across the line, uniting the two platforms. In fact, taking a review of the whole establishment under its present management, it would be difficult to find a place more admirably adapted by construction for its purpose than the salons and hotel at the Swindon station, or persons more nicely adapted to their busy occupation, than the staff employed under the present proprietor. Nor is their task an easy one, when we recollect that the wants of two or three hundred hungry and thirsty souls are to be supplied in less than ten minutes: nothing but perfect aptitude could accomplish so much in so short a time; and here we have a close approximation to perfection, accompanied, too, with undeviating civility, and a moderate tariff or scale of charges, so conspicuous, that "he who runs may read."

So much for the Station-house;—and now let us pay a brief visit to the town of Swindon, and say a few words about the Depôt.

VIEW FROM THE GALLERY OF SWINDON STATION.

The town of Swindon stands on a hill, about a mile south of the station, and commands a fine view over rich valleys, watered by the Cole and Ray, with their numerous tributary streams, bounded by the ridge of chalk which stretches from Hacken, westwards to the Chilterns. It has good, wide streets, with several handsome shops and good stone houses, many buildings having been added since the opening of the Railway; and though it is not a place of much trade or manufacturing industry, yet, being the residence of many persons of independent fortune, having large weekly markets, and being the town where the petty sessions are held, it has an air of bustle and activity, not to be seen in places of a much greater size. The New Town occupies a site north of the older town, and nearer to the station; being well laid out, and on the whole tastefully built by the Company, for the accommodation of the many hundreds of workpeople, clerks, policemen, &c., employed on this portion of the Line. With the exception, however, of the persons employed on and about the Railway, the working population is principally engaged by agricultural pursuits, some few only being employed in the neighbouring stone-quarries. Swindon has two churches,—an old one on the hill, of no great architectural pretensions, and a very handsome new one, a little south of the line, in the decorated English style, with a tower and spire, which, with its adjoining parsonage and school-house, forms a pleasing object from the carriages. There are likewise three dissenting chapels, two banking establishments, a county court office, a mechanics' institute, two good hotels and posting-houses, and between 5,000 and 6,000 inhabitants. The Wilts and Berks canal passes about half a mile north-west of the town; and about a mile south-east is the canal-reservoir, a beautiful lake of seventy acres, most delightfully situated in a picturesque, well-wooded district, and abounding with fish, especially pike, for the amusement of anglers. The principal residences are *Swindon House*, belonging to Ambrose Goddard, Esq., a neat modern-built edifice, with a fine lawn, and extensive attached pleasure-grounds; and the *Hermitage*, occupied by C. A. Wheeler, Esq., which, though of no great magnitude, is prettily situated in grounds extremely well laid out.

A few remarks on the Railway Depôt, and we have done with Swindon. This extensive range of building occupies a space of about eleven acres in the fork between the Bristol and Cheltenham Lines, west of the passenger-station. Its arrangements are altogether on a vast scale; and it has accommodation for about a hundred engines, either in use or undergoing repair. The engine-shed is an oblong structure, 490 feet long, and 72 feet broad; open at each end, and roofed with slate, having standing-room for fifty about engines and tenders, —a certain number of which are kept in constant readiness, with their steam up, to carry on the business of the Company. At right angles to, and abutting against the north side of the shed, is the engine-house, about 300 feet long, and 140 feet wide, divided by two rows of columns into three compartments, where the engines stand in stalls transversely, like horses in a stable, being moved, when required, by a platform which travels on wheels from one end of the building to the other: —it is here, where the engines receive such lighter kinds of repair as can be executed by the engine-men themselves. Further north, again, are work-shops and other offices for the repair of engines, carriages, &c.; and there is also a large building, called the erecting-house, for the reception of new engines while in course of construction. Great activity prevails throughout the depôt; and the works connected with it furnish employment to nearly 2,000 work people.

But, hark! the bell rings, passengers hurry along the platform, carriage-doors slam, the engine groans in impatience at further delay; the steam is turned on, and away we go with lightning speed towards Bath. A mile or two onward, casting our eyes northward, we shall see the fine timber of Viscount Bolingbroke's Park at *Lydiard Tregoze,* (now in the occupancy of C. Orby Wombwell, Esq.,) which comprises some very fine old oaks, besides a handsome sheet of water; and about a mile north-east, is *Lydiard Millicent,* where there is a handsome parsonage, or rather manor-house, in grounds beautifully laid out, belonging to the Rev. Dr. Warneford, a most munificent benefactor to many of the colleges, schools, and other charities in the various towns of Warwickshire, as well as to King's College, London. A few brief minutes' run brings us to the WOOTTON-BASSETT STATION, on the north side of the line near the eighty-third mile-post, a few hundred yards from the ancient town of that name, which was originally called *Wodeton,* and about a century after the conquest became the property of the Bassetts, (a branch of the noble family of the Bassetts of Drayton,) who conferred on it its adjunct name. It was formerly a place of considerable importance, and returned two members to the House of Commons, from 25th Henry the Sixth down to the passing of the Reform Act, when it was disfranchised. For many years past, however, it has had no native

industry, but that connected with the soil; and its melancholy dilapidated appearance tells a sad tale of fallen prosperity never to be restored. It may be here mentioned also, that eight miles to the south lies the secluded village of *Avebury,* or *Abury,* which has particular claims on the antiquary's attention, as containing in and near it the ruins of one of the largest and most interesting of our Druids' temples, surpassing even Stonehenge, in the number and gigantic size of its upright stones, its mound and ditch, and its two avenues. The whole temple is surrounded by a broad trench and mound, within which formerly stood one hundred upright stones, twenty-seven feet apart, and about seventeen feet high, forming together a circle 1400 feet in diameter; and within this again were two circles, each consisting of two double concentric rows, composed of the same number of stones, and similarly arranged. The grand circle had two entrances, consisting of double rows of one hundred upright stones each, placed at equal distances, and extending a mile in length; the one terminating in a double concentric circle of smaller diameter, and the other having a stone larger than the rest at the extremity. Of this vast and most curious structure, however, few traces now remain, inasmuch as the farmers and villagers were allowed, during the whole of the last century, to break down and blow up these venerable monuments, that they might serve for the construction of houses, or as metal for the roads. Dr. Stukely and Sir R. Colt Hoare have very particularly described these ruins, as well as several other cromlechs and tumuli in the neighbourhood, including Silbury-hill, which is 170 feet high, and 1680 feet in circuit, forming, owing to its conical shape and isolated position, conspicuous objects among the low chalk hills of this district. Avebury is only a mile and a half north of Kennet, a place noted for the excellence and strength of its ales.

The Railway on leaving the Wootton-Bassett station descends a rapid incline (about one in sixty) rather more than a mile long, and the traveller will here observe a handsome brick bridge, which crosses the road from Calne to Wootton-Bassett, the Line running for the most part in a deep cutting. In fact, the traveller is now descending into the beautiful valley of "Bath's clear Avon," which the Line crosses for the first time at *Sutton-Benger,* near the ninetieth mile-post, a little previous to which may be perceived, immediately south of the Railway, a bold eminence, called *Bradenstoke Hill.* It may be here mentioned also, that nine miles north-west lies the ancient town of *Malmesbury*, where existed a splendid monastery of Benedictine monks, presided over by a mitred abbot, from the seventh century forward to the dissolution of the religious houses. "The abbey," says Leland, "was a right magnificent thing; where were two steeples, one that had a mighty pyramis, and felle dangerously, and sins was not re-edified. It stode in the middle of the transepture of the church, and was a marke to al the countre about. The othir yet standith; a great square toure at the west ende of the church." The monastery with the church was said to have covered about 45 acres; but nothing beyond foundation-walls now remains, except the nave of the church (still used for divine worship), which exhibits some fine specimens belonging to different eras of architecture, chiefly early English. The town is pleasantly situated on a hill close to the Avon, which nearly encircles it, and is here crossed by six bridges. In the centre of the market-place is an octagonal turreted cross, with flying buttresses, erected probably in the reign of Henry VII. Malmesbury is a place of little trade or manufacturing industry; but it nevertheless sent two members to the House of Commons from the reign of Edward I. to the Reform Act, which deprived it of one of its members, and enlarged the electoral limits: its municipal corporation seems to have become defunct. This town, however, claims the honour of having given birth, among other distinguished persons, to Johannes Scotus, a celebrated schoolman in the middle ages; William of Malmesbury, the historian; and Hobbes, the eminent metaphysician and political writer of the sixteenth and seventeenth centuries.

After a run of eleven miles from Wootton-Bassett, through a country very different from that east of Swindon, undulating and well wooded, watered by the Avon and its small tributaries, we arrive at

CHIPPENHAM STATION,

ninety-four miles from Paddington, on the south bank of the Avon, which nearly surrounds it, and is crossed by a good stone bridge of twenty-two arches, forming a fine approach from the north. The Railway approaches the town on an embankment, elevated considerably above the heads of the houses, and therefore presenting a curious view from the Railway. The town consists of a principal street, with many others of inferior proportions, branching from it in different directions; and near the centre of the whole is the parish church, a very large structure, mostly in the Norman style, comprising a nave, chancel, south aisle, and chapel, with a fine tower and spire at the west end; and it would appear, from the diversities in its style, to have been erected at different periods. In the interior are several monuments well worthy of observation. Chippenham has, also, a handsome modern market-house, over which is a spacious hall or court for public meetings. The woollen and silk trades formerly constituted the staple industry of this place, but we believe the town has now only a very few looms; and it now depends almost entirely upon those markets, and brisk retail trade, which gave it its name in olden time. It has also four large annual fairs for horses, cattle, sheep, and hogs; besides which Chippenham has two banking companies and a savings' bank. Chippenham is both a municipal and parliamentary borough, sending two members to the House of Commons, and governed internally by a mayor and three other aldermen, with twelve councillors. In the neighbourhood of the town are some chalybeate springs, which are probably as available for therapeutic purposes as many others; but as they have ceased to be fashionable, they have, no doubt, lost their virtue!

The view from the carriages on the south side is well represented in the annexed engraving.

CHIPPENHAM

is a place of great antiquity, and, according to the historian Camden, was the country-house of the Saxon kings, which King Alfred by his will bequeathed to his youngest daughter. About three miles from Chippenham are the ancient abbeys of Stanley and Lacock, the latter of which is still the seat of the Talbots. The traveller, however, who has time to tarry at pleasure on his route, will not fail to pay a visit to *Bowood Park*, the seat of the venerable Marquis of Lansdown, a noble demesne of greatly diversified natural features, richly adorned with plantations, and containing within its boundaries eight or nine rich valleys, the broadest of which is partly filled by a noble expansive lake, while on the rising ground above it is the mansion, which, having been built at different periods, is rather an irregular mass, though the principal front is unquestionably handsome, having been built about fifty years ago in the modern Italian villa style. The interior we believe is richly furnished, and contains some beautiful pictures, with other articles of *virtù*. A few words also must be said about *Calne*, which is about five miles from Chippenham, and six from Devizes. It appears to have been a place of great antiquity, and was celebrated in ecclesiastical history as the scene of a controversial conquest gained by Dunstan in behalf of the monks over the secular priors. The town consists of a single clean, principal street, lined by

well-built stone houses. It has one or two woollen mills, and perhaps a few looms; the population is now principally agricultural. Calne, which has sent members to Parliament since the 23rd Edward I., now sends under the Reform Act only one member to the House of Commons.

Ere we leave Chippenham, we must beg leave for a short delay, while we give some account of the leading features on the Frome Branch-line, which diverges from the Main-line at this place. The first stopping-place is the MELKSHAM STATION (rather more than six miles from Chippenham). The town of that name stands on the Avon, which is crossed here by a good stone bridge; and it appears to have been a place of considerable importance in Norman and Saxon times, but during the Tudor dynasty to have fallen into a decay, from which it has been restored only within the last century by its brisk manufactures of broadcloth. This branch of industry, however, has greatly declined owing to the rise of the Yorkshire cloth trade; and, except some tanyards and malthouses, Melksham has few internal resources beyond its fortnightly markets. The town (which has about 7,000 inhabitants) consists principally of one long street, lined somewhat irregularly with good stone houses; and within the parish are two churches, and four or five meeting-houses for Dissenters. About half a mile distant, also, are two mineral-springs (somewhat resembling those of Cheltenham), adjacent to which is a pump-room with hot and cold baths, &c.; and suitable lodging-houses have been erected for the reception of visitors. The proximity of fashionable Bath, however, barely ten miles distant, has sadly hindered the progress of *Melksham Spa.*

A run of five miles and a half further takes us to TROWBRIDGE (11¾ miles from Chippenham), a large market-town of Wiltshire, on the Were, a tributary to the Avon, about a mile south of the Kennet and Avon canal. It stands on the side of a rocky hill, rising pretty sharply from the river, and is irregularly built with narrow streets and old-fashioned houses; but it has a spacious market-place and a large church, consisting of a nave, chancel, two aisles, chapel, and some good painted windows, and a handsome tower and spire at the west-end. The staple trade of Trowbridge and its vicinity has consisted in the manufacture of woollen-cloths ever since the reign of Henry VIII., and it still produces a large quantity of cassimeres, kerseys, and certain qualities of broad-cloth. This trade, however, has been greatly impaired by the rising importance of Bradford, and other towns in the West-riding of Yorkshire. Trowbridge has a population of about 12,000 persons.

About four miles from Trowbridge is the large and ancient town of *Bradford*, on the Lower Avon, here crossed by two bridges. It is very well built, and comprises some handsome houses, with a very fine old church, well worthy of a visit. The chief staple of the town, as of most others in this district, is woollen-cloth, especially the finest qualities of broad-cloth, for dyeing which the water of the Avon is said to be particularly favourable. More recently, also, a very extensive Indian-rubber manufactory has been established by S. Moulton, Esq., on the Kingston estate, which gives employment to 400 or 500 persons of both sexes. Bradford has between 11,000 and 12,000 inhabitants.

A ride of ten miles further takes us to the FROME STATION, the terminus of the Branch-line, close to the parliamentary borough of *Frome*, in Somersetshire, on the river of the same name, eleven miles south-east of Bath. It stands on an acclivity bordering on Selwood Forest, and rising abruptly from the river, which is here spanned by a bridge of five arches; and, though it has many narrow streets, it is on the whole well built and very clean, having a good modern market-place, and a large parish church in the decorated-English style, with a fine tower, and spire 150 feet high, and some interesting monuments, including the tomb of the celebrated non-juring Bishop Ken. It is to this church that the notorious Mr. Bennett has lately been presented by the Marchioness of Bath, and inducted by the bishop of the diocese, against the urgent protest of the inhabitants. There are two other churches within the parish, which also comprises five or six dissenting chapels. The woollen manufacture forms here, as at Trowbridge, the ancient staple of the town, and furnishes the chief employment of the inhabitants; the goods made here consisting chiefly of the finer qualities of broad-cloth and kerseymeres. Livery-cloths, carriage-linings, and hats also are made here; besides which, cards for dressing wool are manufactured, though to a much less extent than formerly, when it supplied them to the greater part of England. Frome was erected into a parliamentary borough by the Reform Act, since the passing of which it has returned one member to the House of Commons;—the present member being the Hon. Robert Boyle, son of the Earl of Cork. The neighbourhood is extremely fertile and picturesque, comprising many old family mansions and estates, including among others *Longleat*, the noble demesne of the Marquis of Bath. The mansion is an uniform quadrangular structure, of large proportions, and Grecian architecture, built wholly of freestone, and the park within the plantations is about fifteen miles in circumference.

Having thus briefly sketched the Frome Branch-line, let us onward towards Bath.

On leaving Chippenham, the Railway is carried by a viaduct over the Malmesbury-road; and thence five short miles bring us to the CORSHAM STATION, somewhat more than ninety-eight miles from Paddington. The town, which is not seen from the Railway, has a handsome church with a very richly carved stone-screen, and it had formerly two religious houses; for it was a place of some note in the time of the Saxons. Its woollen manufacture was at one time of considerable importance; but retail trade and agricultural pursuits now form the staple employment of its inhabitants, who may amount to about 3,000. Not far distant, on the north side of the Line, is *Corsham Park*, the seat of Lord Methuen, whose family have held the property for the last two centuries.

And now, timid lady-travellers, screw up your nerves for a rush through the Box Tunnel. No,— not this first one:—it is only a short preliminary taste, before we enter the real stone-cut gallery beneath the Box-hill, which forms a striking feature with its rugged surface from all parts of the surrounding country, and is interesting as having been one of the principal quarries for the erections in Bath. We here give a very careful representation of

THE ENTRANCE TO THE BOX TUNNEL.

A short description of this great engineering-work may not be uninteresting. Its entrance from the east is through a deep cutting with vertical sides hewn out of the rock; the arch is semi-circular, formed of rusticated work, and springing from upright sides; and on either side is a projecting pier. As respects the rocks through which the tunnel penetrates, we have already remarked (p. 12), that it traverses in succession the great or middle (sometimes called the *upper*) oolite, so well known as the Bath building-stone,—then two thick beds of fuller's-earth and light clay,—after that the lower or lesser oolite,—lastly, a blue marl-stone or shale, separating the oolites from the lias beneath; and it is in this stratum that the tunnel terminates, and pursues its course all the way to Bath. The Box-tunnel is 3,195 yards, or about a mile and three-quarters long, lined nearly throughout with brickwork, and ventilated by six shafts, each 25 feet in diameter, and varying from 70 to 300 feet in depth; the whole run through it being a rapid incline westward. This tunnel, it may be interesting to know, occupied two years and a half in formation, involving the labour of excavating no less than 414,000 cubic yards of earth and stone, chiefly the latter; besides the construction of 54,000 cubic yards of masonry and brickwork, with a consumption of more than thirty millions

of bricks. A ton of gunpowder was used weekly in blasting, and a ton of candles for lighting the labourers, who averaged more than a thousand during the whole undertaking.

The Box Station stands close to the west end of the tunnel; but we shall not tarry an instant here, except to call attention to the pretty church of the village of *Box*, on the south of the Line. Soon after emerging from the tunnel, the Line enters into the main valley of the Avon, after its return from its southward meandering; and from this point onwards all the way to Bristol, the scenery is most beautiful, exhibiting all the characteristics of the cultivation, whether pasture or arable, peculiar to North Somersetshire,—fine meadows and rich corn-fields, both sadly overrun with umbrageous elms, which, with all their picturesque features, are specially prejudicial to the land and the farmers' interests,—no slight matters in these days of non-protection. *Bathford Bridge*, over which the Line crosses the Avon, now a wide and handsome-looking stream, is a beautiful structure, having a single elliptical arch, 54 feet wide and 27 feet high, met on either side by an embankment. The village of *Bathford* stands on the left bank of the river; and the church has a very pretty tower in the perpendicular style, with a curious pulpit of the Elizabethan era, and a good Norman north door. Look, however, on the opposite, that is, on the northern side, and you will presently see the beautiful perpendicular tower of *Bath-easton* church. This sacred building is well worthy of a visit; and to the lover of our native literature it possesses a melancholy interest, as containing the tomb of the Rev. J. J. Conybeare, formerly Anglo-Saxon professor at Oxford, and brother of the celebrated geologist of the same name.

And now we are approaching Bath—"the Queen of the West;" nor, as we rapidly drive onward, is it possible to refuse our admiration to the beautifully green and rich meadows that surround us on either side, profusely fringed with graceful timber-trees of various kinds and hues, beyond which, as the land rises, we still see all the smiling indications of a most productive soil far away up to the point of the horizon. The Railway, as it approaches Bath, lies at the foot of *Claverton Downs*; and now also may be seen *Salisbury* and *Banner Downs* with their ancient entrenchments. Before entering Bath, also, we shall pass the village of Bath-hampton, with its exceedingly pretty church and perpendicular tower: this place is now, by the progress of building, almost united to Bath.

G

CHAPTER VI.

BATH, GENERAL DESCRIPTION—ABBEY AND CHURCHES—BATHS AND PUMP-ROOM—ASSEMBLY-ROOMS AND THEATRE—BEAU NASH—VICINITY OF BATH—TWERTON—NEWTON PARK—KEYNSHAM AND BITTON—BRISTOL, GENERAL DESCRIPTION—ST. MARY REDCLIFFE—CLIFTON AND THE HOT WELLS.

THE Great Western Railway enters Bath through a deep cutting close to Sydney Gardens, a favourite promenade and place of amusement in this gay city, which the Line, instead of injuring, contributes not a little to embellish. Beyond this the Line passes beneath several houses and a street, sweeping round to the Poulteney-road on an embankment, and over a beautiful stone viaduct bridge, forty feet above the Avon, and then almost immediately enters

THE BATH STATION,

a principal and very important stage on the Line, 107 miles from Paddington, 30 miles from Swindon, and 12 miles from Bristol. Its general architecture is debased Elizabethan, with Gothic windows, and Romanesque embellishments; the principal front being flanked by curved wing-walls, to form a circular carriage-sweep. The platform is covered from end to end; and its roof is somewhat peculiar, having a span of 60 feet without either buttress or tie of any description either vertical or horizontal: the effect is unique in its way, nor can anything be better suited to the general appearance. Every Bristol train, up or down, stops at Bath; and the arrangements in every respect are most complete.

Of all the cities of Europe, Rome and Edin-burgh excepted, Bath presents, perhaps, the most striking panoramic spectacle which a traveller can behold as he approaches it for the first time. The city lies at the bottom of the Avon valley, encompassed by a triple circle of hills rising in successive terraces one above another, beatling over the city beneath; and from whatever point of the old or new city (that down in the valley, or that which climbs the hills in various directions) the visitor casts his glance around, some height or steep presents itself, invested with its own peculiar beauties, natural and acquired. Being all of them portions of the great oolitic series, their shapes are gracefully rounded or waving; and whether we trace the steep ascent of *Claverton* on the east, up to the table-land on its summit, 600 feet above the sea, or turn round to the loftier range of *Lansdown*, 813 feet high, to the north-west, passing for that purpose over the lovely eminence of Bathwick in the north-east, we find every part of the horizon occupied by some picturesque elevation, once barren and all but inaccessible, though now easy of access, and teaming with a busy population.

BATH FROM BEACHEN CLIFF.

In the midst of these hills, all bearing distinctive names, stands the old city of Bath, only forty feet above the Avon, which, as it comes from Bathhampton in the far north-east, is seen winding and turning as its descends into the level valley, skirting with its right or northern bank first the old and then the new city, and finally quitting the latter, around the south-western base of Lansdown hill, enters the rich meads and pastures westward, among which it wanders, ere it reaches Kenysham, on its way to Bristol. On a narrow tongue of land, formed by a sudden bend of the river from its north and south to a north-west course, is the Old Bath, said to have been the bath of the Romans, with its hot springs occupying the centre; and near to them is the celebrated Abbey Church, and the no less famed *Orange Grove*, with the *North* and *South Parade*, and the *Pump-room*. Still, however old this part of the city may be, yet it has been in almost all its parts most tastefully modernised and embellished; and many low, crazy tenements have consequently disappeared, while several of the streets have been widened and made more regular. Northward of this section of Bath is that portion, including *Milsom-street*, leading to *Queen-square*, and the *Circus*, a fine assemblage of spacious mansions rich in architectural decoration—the creation of the two Woods, father and son, to whom Bath is indebted more than to any one else for its grandeur and uniformity of its buildings. West of the Circus again the visitor will soon emerge on one of the finest amphitheatres that Europe presents—the *Royal Crescent*, arranged on the slope of a hill, and commanding a most extensive view of the city, *Victoria Park*, one of the finest pleasure grounds in England, immediately at his feet. The Crescent is flanked on its western side by the handsome and straight line of *Marlborough Buildings*. Higher still we shall come to what is emphatically the *New Town*, the work of the last thirty years, which comprises *St. James's Square; Norfolk, Cavendish, Somerset,* and *Lansdown Crescents; Camden Crescent,* and *Camden Place,* all more or less, but especially the last, commanding fine panoramic views of the city beneath, fully proving the truth of the poet's lines:

"—— what a goodly prospect spreads around,
Of hills and dales and woods and lawns and spires,
The glitt'ring town, and gilded stream, till all
The stretching landscape into smoke decays!"

Bath has also a fourth region, known under the general name of *Bathwick*, separated from the city by the Avon, and presenting, as it were, a new town, strongly contrasting by its exquisitely-finished buildings, magnificent streets, and open squares, with the oldest part of the city, to which it lies immediately opposite. It may here be mentioned also, that the Avon, as it meanders through Bath, is crossed by no less than *nine* bridges; three of stone, two of cast-iron, three on the suspension-principle, and one (connected with the railway) of kyanised timber.

Having thus generally described the appearance and arrangement of Bath, we shall now furnish a more detailed account of the public buildings and institutions, that are so abundant and so remarkable in this beautiful city. We shall first speak of the churches; and among these the first place is justly due to the *Cathedral*, or Abbey church.

BATH ABBEY.

The present edifice, which the best judges usually deem one of the last legitimate specimens of orna-mental-English church-architecture, owes its origin to Oliver King, bishop of this see in the reign of Henry VII.; and it appears to have been some-what more than a century in course of erection (being begun in 1499, and completed in 1606). The exterior generally has few features to call forth any intensity of admiration, having a meagre,

unfinished appearance; and the central tower, like the church itself, exhibits unmistakeable indications of the decay of art. The western front of the church, however, which is represented in our engraving, is exceedingly curious, and though now much worn by the action of the atmosphere, must at some past time have been a beautiful object. The story goes, that the ladders and figures represent a vision of the above prelate, wherein he saw the Trinity, with angels ascending and descending a ladder, and calling upon him to build the present church on the site of an older and decayed one belonging to a Benedictine monastery. The western window is one of excellent proportions; and underneath it is the principal entrance to the church through a richly carved door, bearing the arms of Bishop Montague, impaled with those of the see. The interior is remarkably light and elegant, and the roof would be good, were it real; but unhappily, with the exception of the ornamental part, which is stone, the whole is of miserable lath and plaster; and this, too, where stone might have been had for the carrying! A modern and very beautiful screen, by Blore, separates the nave from the choir; and under his directions, we believe, much was done to remove monumental disfigurements and other eye-sores. The interior, however, is far too glaring to give persons any notion of the " dim religious light" that is considered so desirable a feature in the solemn temples of the Almighty. Of monu-ments their name is Legion; for the friends of almost every person of any distinction seem to have considered it a duty to put up some bust, tablet, or memorial; whence, no doubt, the words of the epigram—

> These walls, adorned with monument or bust,
> Show how Bath waters serve to lay the dust.

The most prominent monument in the church is an altar-tomb of the pious Bishop Montague, the liberal benefactor to the church at its restoration, at the commencement of the seventeenth century. It stands under an arch, dividing the nave from the north aisle. The bishop is represented in his pon-tifical habit, with his hands raised in the attitude of prayer. The lady of Sir William Waller the parlia-mentarian, also Quin the actor, Melmoth the trans-lator of Cicero, Beau Nash, Malthus the political economist, &c., are interred here, and represented by monuments of one sort or another, but in very questionable taste.

The finest of the *old* parish churches is *St. James's*, which, however, was built only in the middle of the last century, and in the Roman style; the present elegant belfry-tower (150 feet high) having been recently added. *St. Michael's*, at the top of High Street, is a singularly beautiful modern imitation of the early English style, and has an airy, pierced spire of admirable proportions, 182 feet high: this church occupies the site of three or four successive structures, the first of which was built probably during the fifteenth century. *St. Mary's Bathwick*, near Sydney Gardens, is a good modern example of the ornamented-English, and the interior, which is very extensive, is a fair imitation of that beautiful, but licentious style; it has a good tower, about 120 feet high, with decorated pinnacles at the four angles. *Walcot Church*, *Christ Church* in Montpelier Row, *St. Stephen's* on the Lansdown Road, *St. Saviour's* on the London Road, and *St. Matthew's*, are the other principal churches; besides which, Bath has fourteen or fifteen chapels-of-ease, a Roman Catholic chapel, and about twenty meeting-houses, for the various classes of dissenters. Of the latter, perhaps, the most celebrated and most frequented is that in Argyle Street, where the Rev. William Jay has officiated upwards of sixty years. In connection also with the churches and chapels, we may call attention to the modern cemeteries of Bath, which have entirely removed any necessity for intermural interments. The oldest of these is that connected with Walcot church, immediately adjacent to the rectory; this was formed in 1840, and comprises about a hundred catacombs cut in the rock below the street-level. The principal burying-place of the city, however, is the *Abbey Cemetery* on the south side of the Avon, leading towards Claverton Downs: it is a present in perpetuity to the Abbey church by the Honourable and Reverend W. J. Brodrick, the justly respected incumbent of the mother-church of Bath. This cemetery, consecrated in 1844, was the last work in ornamental gardening ever executed by the late celebrated Mr. Loudon; and apart from the internal beauties with which his art has invested it, the grounds command one of the finest and most expansive views that are to be found of the city of Bath. The *Walcot Cemetery*, on the southern brow of Lansdown, is of still more recent formation, having been opened only four years; and perhaps no spot could have been selected of more picturesque beauty, or more completely adapted for the purposes of sepulture. The ground was presented by the Duchess of Hamilton; and the first body deposited was that of the celebrated William Beckford, author of "Vathek," the father of the Duchess, and the former proprietor of the Lansdown estate. The entrance to the cemetery

is by a splendidly decorated archway, surmounted by a campanile crowned with an octagonal Grecian lantern, 130 feet high.

We shall now describe what constitutes the chief glory of Bath, and the true source of its long-continued prosperity—THE BATHS AND HOT SPRINGS. The springs are situated at a very short distance from each other, and are no doubt branches of one grand reservoir, whence are supplied the five baths of the city. The remains of ancient and very splendid baths, found in digging the foundations for the present King's bath, make it quite certain that the Romans (a people notorious for their love of bathing) largely availed themselves of the advantages offered by these thermal springs; and from that time to the present these springs have been more or less resorted to, with the view either of restoring health or gratifying the feelings. Numerous, but unsatisfactory conjectures have been formed on the causes of the great heat evolved by these waters. We shall content ourselves with stating the facts: The King's bath is supplied with 126 gallons per minute of water having a temperature of 114° Fahrenheit, and the temperature of the hot bath is about three degrees higher. The water is transparent and colourless, inodorous, somewhat metallic, but by no means unpleasant to the taste; and if kept for some hours it deposits a slight orange sediment. We here subjoin the results of Mr. Phillips's analysis of a quart of water taken from the hot spring :—

Solid.	Sulphate of lime	18.	grains.
	Chloride of sodium	6.6	,,
	Sulphate of soda	3,	,,
	Carbonate of lime	1.6	,,
	Silica	.4	,,
	Oxide of iron	a trace	
		29.6	grains.
Gaseous.	Carbonic acid	2.4	cub. inches.

The general indications for the use of these medicinal waters are in cases where a general stimulus is required, especially in those of a chronic character, including gout, rheumatism, scrofula, and various kinds of eruptive diseases, as well as those of the digestive organs. The reader, however, who desires further information on the Bath waters will do well to peruse Dr. Granville's fourth volume of the "Spas of England," which contains one of the most interesting accounts of Bath and its thermal springs that we have yet met with. The *King's Bath*, built on the site of the old Roman thermo, is situated about 120 feet west of the Abbey church, being sixty-six feet long, forty feet wide, and containing when full 1,460 hogsheads of water: it is provided with seats for bathers, and a Doric colonnade on one side affords shelter from the weather. The *Queen's Bath* (which is, in fact, only a separated portion of the last-mentioned) forms a quadrangle of twenty feet in each direction, and contains about 250 hogsheads: connected with it are several handsome private baths. The best private baths, however, are those on the opposite side of Stall Street, attached to the *Hot Bath:* these are equal in comfort and elegance to anything to be found even at the Continental Spas. The other bath-establishments are the *Cross Bath*, the *Tepid Swimming Bath* (containing 670 hogsheads of water), and the *Kingston Baths* in Church Street, belonging to Earl Manvers, one of the chief ground-landlords in Bath.

Any account of the mineral springs of Bath, however, would be very imperfect without some description of the *Pump-room*, the fashionable afternoon lounge of the *élite* of the visitors, for whose amusement a well-appointed band daily discourses excellent music. This saloon is sixty feet long, fifty-six wide, and thirty-four high, independently of the semicircular recesses at either end, and is adorned with numerous busts and pictures, including BEAU NASH, the *arbiter elegantiarum* and master of the ceremonies in Bath for many years in the early part of the last century, a man who, possessing little or no talent, exercised a sway so ridiculously powerful, as to reflect little credit on the good sense either of the visitors or citizens, who submitted to his caprices. The *Assembly-rooms* in which Nash figured, as the absolute king of folly and fashion, were burnt down about thirty years ago: the present were built at enormous cost by the younger Wood, and contain a lofty ball-room upwards of a hundred feet long, with two card-rooms and a tea-room, forming altogether one of the finest suite of saloons in the kingdom. Bath has also a very handsome *Theatre*, with two tiers of boxes, besides private boxes; and the Bath company has always ranked as the first in the provinces, not without justice; for a great proportion of the leading actors and opera-singers of the day had, previously to treading the metropolitan boards, tried their 'prentice hands at Bath. There are three or four clubs, in humble imitation of the gigantic London establishments, several reading-rooms, libraries, &c., with an Athenæum, literary institution, &c., admirably suited to enable visitors to pass their time usefully as well as agreeably in-doors; while, for those who prefer out-door amusement, combined with gentle exercise, there are the *Sydney Gardens* eastward,

and the *Victoria Park* at the west end of the new town. The former, opened at the close of the last century, occupy an area of about sixteen acres, and are beautifully laid out with well-grown trees and thickly-wooded copses, rich flowery parterres, broad well-gravelled promenades, and secluded sylvan walks well-sheltered from the sun: fêtes and galas are frequently celebrated here during the summer *à la* Vauxhall, and a band plays every evening. Victoria Park is a fine well-planted expanse of some 300 acres, formed about twenty years ago on a piece of ground that had long been a common field: the entrance adjoins the Queen's Parade close to the Royal Crescent; and just within the gates is a handsome obelisk erected in 1837 in honour of her Majesty, called the *Victoria Column*. The drives through the park are ample in point of extent, and well planned to furnish fine and varied views both of Bath and the neighbouring country.

Bath has enjoyed municipal privileges since the time of Richard I.; and its corporation has for some centuries been one of the wealthiest and most important in the provincial districts. Under the Municipal Reform Act the city is divided into seven wards, and governed by a mayor and thirteen other aldermen, and forty-two councillors. This ancient city also has sent two members to Parliament since the reign of Edward I. : nor has the Reform Act interfered with this privilege, as the city still returns two members to the House of Commons. The *Guildhall*, in which the corporation and judicial business of the city is transacted, stands in the High Street, not far from the Abbey and Orange Grove; it has several courts, large offices, &c., on the ground floor, and above is a finely decorated banquetting-room eighty feet long, forty wide, and thirty feet high, the walls of which are covered with portraits of royal and celebrated personages. The *Markets* form a sort of wings to the Guildhall, extending also behind it; and perhaps in no town of the kingdom will be found better and more abundant supplies of every kind of *comestibles*, meat, fish, poultry, butter, vegetables, and fruit, all at prices proverbial for cheapness. As for the trade of Bath, it almost exclusively depends on its visitors, who in some seasons add as many as 15,000 persons to the permanent population, at the same time greatly enriching the town by the profits attendant on the supply of their numerous aristocratic requirements.

Bath has numerous educational and benevolent institutions, hospitals, &c.; which we have no space to particularise even by name; but a few words must be said about *Kingswood* and *Partis Colleges*, as they are very conspicuous features in the scenery, from whatever part Bath may be viewed. The former is a very large structure of rich Tudor architecture, conspicuously placed near the top of Lansdown, being built in the form of the letter H, and having a handsome central tower rising eighty-two feet above the building, which, besides theatres, lecture-rooms, and a fine hall, has accommodation for 150 students, the sons of Wesleyan-Methodist preachers. *Partis College*, which stands on Newbridge Hill, close to the upper Bristol Road, was built by Mrs. Partis, in 1827, to provide a comfortable home for thirty reduced and aged ladies—the widows or daughters of clergymen of the established church. The building has a handsome appearance from the road; and attached to it is a chapel, in which service is regularly performed by the chaplain of the institution.

The neighbourhood of Bath abounds with beautiful walks and drives; but the invalid, or one not accustomed to long, laborious climbing of hill-sides, will prefer hiring a vehicle to visit the splendid scenery that awaits his admiration. On the slope of Coombe Down southward is *Prior Park*, now appropriated to the purposes of a Roman Catholic College; and a very handsome structure it is, commanding a fine view both of Bath and Lansdown beyond, through the deep glen of Widcomb; the hills around commanding the whole valley from Bath-easton on one side, to the river valley below Weston on the other. A romantic lane, called Pope's walk, from the frequent visits of that poet to Bishop Warburton, when he held Prior Park, leads pretty directly down to the city. *Hinton*, *Philip's Norton*, *Wellow*, and *Combehay*, all in the same direction, are well worthy of an excursion; and another, almost equally interesting, may be made to *Claverton Downs*, the village of *Claverton*, the *Dundas Aqueduct*, and the ruins of *Farleigh-Montford*, the ancient seat of the De Montfords and Hungerfords. Another beautiful drive is to the secluded valley of *Charlcombe*, on the north side of Lansdown; and when the excursionist has attained the summit of that hill, a view will burst on him that has few in England to equal it. On the east he will behold in the far distance the hills of Wiltshire from Salisbury Plain, embracing the Marlborough Downs and their continuations as far as Devizes, on the north-east and north the high lands of Gloucester and Worcester; while, looking westward, he will behold the lofty hills beyond Abergavenny, the well-wooded Mon-

mouth bank of the Severn, with the Welsh coast about Cardiff, and the broad æstuary of the Bristol Channel, including lovely Clifton and smoky Bristol, with the Mendip Hills closing the view southward. But Bath has detained us already much too long: and so with some reluctance we must bid her adieu.

Behold us now once more in motion toward Bristol. The skew timber bridge is crossed, and the Wells road, too; and now we are passing over a viaduct that commands a fine view of the western terraces of Bath. The TWERTON STATION is a mile and a half from Bath, and adjoins a village principally supported by a large manufactory of broad-cloth, generally reputed to be in a prosperous condition. Twerton, also, contains the cottage where Henry Fielding lived in his earlier days, and where he wrote his first and best work, "Tom Jones." The Twerton Tunnel occurs soon after leaving the station; after which the Line goes under the Bath road, (which is carried over by an oblique iron bridge,) and enters the meadows of Newton-St.-Loe, the property of W. H. Gore Langton, Esq., the owner of *Newton Park*,—a beautiful, well-wooded demesne, with every variety of park scenery, and a fine lake;—but few there be that are allowed to survey its beauties. A Norman ivy-clad tower stands in the immediate vicinity of the mansion, and is traced as far back as the reign of Henry I. The house is quite plain,—unworthy, in fact, of so fine a park, and not creditable to so wealthy a landed-proprietor;—the gardens, however, are well worth a visit, as being devoted to all kinds of exotic plants, as well as the choicest productions that have been naturalised in our climate.

Passing Weston and Kelston, (the old seat of the Harringtons, on the north side,) we arrive at the SALTFORD STATION, nearly five miles from Bath; and immediately west of it the Line enters a lias cutting, through which it passes, till it reaches the KEYNSHAM STATION, about two miles further, situated about half-way between *Keynsham* and *Bitton*. The former of these places is a considerable town, built on an elevated rock, and consisting of a single long street, remarkable for its curious domestic architecture: it has a very handsome church, with a fine tower and some curious monuments; and the people are principally employed in malting, linen-weaving, and spinning wool for the more prosperous clothing towns. As for Bitton, it is remarkable for some interesting British remains, and for a noble church of Norman and early

English architecture. The Railway, after leaving Keynsham Station, speedily enters the coal-strata through a country as rugged and uninviting as the previous part of the journey through the Avon Valley had been smiling and pleasant. Here galleries and tunnels cut in the rock form the passage of the train for about two miles and a half, the most disagreeable part of the whole journey; but at length, about two miles from the Terminus, the Railway enters a level plain formed of the new red-sandstone, covered by alluvium, and after crossing the Avon, enters the western suburb of Bristol, and dashes into the most magnificent station yet existing on the Line,

THE BRISTOL TERMINUS.

The city of BRISTOL is situated in a valley, eight miles from the mouth of the Avon, near its confluence with the Frome on the north bank of the former. Close to the river side is the ancient city, bounded on one side by the Avon, on another by the Frome, and on a third by the ancient moat of the castle. This part contains some very ancient houses and narrow streets, in which the upper stories often project considerably beyond the line of the ground floor; but many of the streets have of late been widened, and otherwise improved in appearance. The highest parts of the city are those called *St. Michael's Hill* and *Kingsdown*, which are about 200 feet above the level of the lowest street.

The streets, which should be carefully examined by the lover of mediæval architecture, (for they contain some fine specimens,) are well worthy of a day's stroll through them. As for the modern, and less interesting parts, they are mostly lined with good houses; and there are several spacious squares surrounded by elegant buildings. The progress of building till lately was towards the west, and many of the principal inhabitants reside at Clifton, which we shall describe—anon.

Bristol has about twenty-three churches connected with the establishment, and between thirty and forty dissenting places of worship. Some of the former present beautiful specimens of ancient English ecclesiastical architecture, the finest perhaps being the tower of St. Stephen's, celebrated for the decorated elegance of its summit, and the Church of St. Mary Redcliffe, to which latter much interest is attached, from the circumstance of its being the church where Chatterton,

> The marvellous boy,
> Who perished in his pride,

said he discovered the manuscripts of Rowley's poems. The muniment-room over the porch, and the chest in which he said he discovered the said poems, will be visited by all interested in the creations of this marvellous genius. *St. Mary Redcliffe*, of which we here give a sketch, is said to be the finest parish church in the kingdom, strongly resembling a cathedral. It was begun in 1292 by Simon de Burton, and was completed in 1377 by William Canynges, senior. The church contains a monument of Sir William Penn, the father of the founder of Pennsylvania. To the right of the organ-loft is a mural tablet to the memory of a much-beloved Bristol worthy, Sir F. Freeling, who, from having been an apprentice in the post-office of his native town, rose to the highest position in the General Post-office, which he held for forty years, and died a baronet at the age of seventy-two, leaving a name worthy of the highest honour.

ST. MARY REDCLIFFE.

The *Cathedral Church* in College Green is a beautiful structure in the form of a cross, and presenting specimens of the various styles of English architecture. The whole length is 175 feet, the breadth of the transept 128 feet, the height of the tower 140 feet, and the breadth of the nave and aisles 73 feet. The entrance to the choir is through an empannelled screen, covered with rich carvings. Some of the side chapels are very beautiful, and contain monuments of the founder, of several abbots and bishops, of Mrs. Draper, the "Eliza" of Sterne, of Mrs. Mason, and of Lady Hesketh, the amiable friend of Cowper.

In some of the streets will be found some capital specimens of the domestic architecture of the middle ages, lying oddly enough cheek by jowl with new raw-looking structures of brick and mortar. "To what base uses may we come at last!" Thus we find in the Pithay, one of the finest old Tudor mansions in the occupation of a slopseller. In one of the principal thoroughfares, also, is a fine old gable building, now used as a bank. In fact, it has been very truly and happily remarked respecting Bristol, that we there see "nodding old gable fronts with their upper stories projecting over the pathway, side by side with modern erections of first-rate finish and stability:— we pass from a noble street in two minutes to the centre of a filthy court; and we find princely wealth and gin-sodden poverty huddled together in close contact."

Among the public buildings the *Exchange* in Corn Street is at once the finest and most important. It is a handsome and spacious edifice, in the Corinthian order of architecture; and the Assembly Rooms in Princes Street are of the same character as the Exchange. The *Victoria Rooms* at the top of Park Street, intended for public assemblies, present a very handsome exterior. The *Theatre* was erected in 1766, and is open for performances during the winter. There are several most valuable literary and scientific institutions in the town. The City Library, founded by Robert Redwood in 1615, has had accessions of books at various times, and now contains upwards of 15,000 volumes. There is also the Bristol Library Society. A Medical Library was founded in 1831, and is well supported by the profession.

The *Bristol Institution* is a handsome building in Park Street. It has a reading-room, a small library, and a museum. The museum comprises a very fine collection of ancient and modern works of art;—among them Baily's celebrated statue of Eve at the fountain, and a complete set of casts from the Æginetan marbles. Courses of lectures are given here.

AN OLD HOUSE IN BRISTOL.

Among the charitable institutions of Bristol, we must not forget the *Infirmary*, founded in 1753. It is a large building, with accommodation for 200 in-patients. The income of the institution is £7,000 per annum. The *Bristol General Hospital* is a smaller establishment.

Bristol possesses considerable historical interest. It was a place of considerable importance during the Roman occupancy, and it is supposed that Vespasian founded the Roman station *Abona* at Sea Mills, upon the Avon, below Westbury-upon-Trym. Its consequence as a port dates from the time of Canute (1017); and to the early part of the Norman period the addition of a second wall around the town is ascribed. From the Domesday-book we gather the actual condition of the town at the time of the Norman Conquest; that it was a royal burgh, the tenants holding immediately under the king; and the local government vested in a prepositor or chief magistrate, the officer of that name at the time of the conquest being Hardyng, a wealthy merchant of the town, and the founder of the Berkeley family. One, in particular, who greatly contributed to the growth of Bristol as a trading port, was William Canynges, the most celebrated merchant of his day, and the reputed founder of St. Mary Redcliffe, who was mayor of Bristol at the time of Edward IV.'s succession to the crown. It is also recorded that he employed,

for the space of eight years, 800 seamen, and 100 artificers daily. In his old age he became a priest in the college of Westbury, which he had founded.

For some time after this the prosperity of Bristol declined; but its fortunes were revived by the spirit and energy of that celebrated discoverer Sebastian Cabot, a native of the town, and one of the most distinguished maritime discoverers of his day. Bristol, too, must have had great repute as a sea-port; for we find that the first vessel which touched the shores of the American continent was the " Matthew," of Bristol; and the earliest letters patent on record for the discovery and colonisation of new lands were granted to three merchants of Bristol, in conjunction with three Portuguese. In the reign of James I., Newfoundland was colonised from Bristol; and from this period down to the year 1787 the progress of the shipping trade was sure and steady. Since the close of the American war, however, Bristol may be said to have lost her claim to be considered the second commercial port in the kingdom, being gradually more and more eclipsed by the rising importance of Liverpool.

EXTERIOR OF BRISTOL STATION.

CLIFTON forms the western continuation of Bristol, and within the last 60 years has risen from a comparatively insignificant village to a beautiful city, lined with noble streets and lordly mansions, bearing evidence to the wealth, prosperity, and good taste of its proprietors. It is sublimely situated on the summit of a precipitous cliff, beetling over the Avon, and commanding delicious views of all the country around, including the highly cultivated lands of Somersetshire and south Gloucestershire, with the western portion of Bristol. The navigable Avon beneath, winds through a chasm between the bases of this and the opposite cliff, which shoots perpendicularly upwards, to a height so nearly even with that of Clifton, as to leave little doubt that the fissure was formed by some violent convulsion. The rocks are of limestone or marble of curious shades, from light red to brown, and gray to blue, great quantities of it being annually burnt into lime. Clifton possesses a remarkably mild and balmy atmosphere, entitling it in some measure to the name of the Montpelier of England; and it is peculiarly suited to persons of debilitated and delicate constitutions, for whom also the *Bristol Hot Wells* down on the river bank some hundred feet below are especially well adapted.

These waters contain chiefly nitrate of magnesia, carbonate of lime, sulphate of lime, chloride of sodium, and sulphate of soda, as well as a considerable quantity of the carbonic acid and nitrogen gases; being recommended mostly for consumptions, weakness of the lungs, and all cases attended with hectic fever and heat.

The Hot Wells are connected with Clifton by the *Zigzag*, or winding artificial walk made in the cliff, which leads by gentle declivities to the summit, furnishing on the ascent prospects of exquisite beauty and grandeur, constantly increasing the higher we go, in extent and sublimity. We may here also mention that not far from the summit of this rock a good view is obtained of the buttresses at *St. Vincent's Rocks*, intended some day or other to support a suspension bridge over the Avon. Such is a very general description of Clifton: more particulars will be given in our Illustrated Guide to the Bristol and Exeter Railway.

CHAPTER VII.

Purton—Minety—Tetbury Road—Cirencester, Oakley Grove, and the Old Roman Roads—Brimscombe—Stroud, its Valley and Mills—Gloucester, its Cathedral and Port—Cheltenham and its Spa.

THE country for the first few miles, after the Cheltenham Line leaves Swindon, exhibits few features of difference from that on the Main Line from Didcot to the Junction. The Purton Road Station connects the Railway with the parliamentary borough, but very insignificant town, of Cricklade. Next comes the Minety Station, about eighty-five miles from London, near which is *Minety House*, the property of W. T. Keene, Esq. ; and about four miles to the west is *Charlton House*, the estate of the Earl of Suffolk. Five miles further take us to the Tetbury Road Station, six miles from *Tetbury*, a clean respectable town built on a hill, with good stone-houses, a large market-house, fine church with spire, and about 3,500 inhabitants, employed in wool-stapling, retail trade, and agricultural pursuits.

It is here that the Railway sends off a branch three miles in length to *Cirencester*, one of the most considerable towns in East Gloucestershire, and well deserving of description.

Cirencester has the appearance of a neat country-town, in good condition, somewhat increasing in buildings, and having altogether an air of opulence and prosperity. It has a magnificent church in the early English style, with later additions, and has a nave and choir with five chapels, and a noble embattled tower 132 feet high, ornamented with pinnacles and statues; the east and west windows are filled with painted glass, and the church contains many very curious sepulchral brasses; so that, on the whole, it is eminently worthy of a visit. The parish possesses numerous valuable charities, including a free grammar-school, founded by Bishop Ruthall in the reign of Henry the Seventh, which gave the rudiments of learning to the celebrated Dr. Jenner, the discoverer of vaccination. Cirencester, though formerly much engaged in the wool-trade, and one of the largest wool-markets in England, has only one cloth-mill and one carpet-factory ; indeed, it depends at present almost wholly on its retail trade for the supply of the landed gentry round, and on its weekly markets. Cirencester has a population of about 8,000 persons, and has sent two members to the British Parliament ever since the reign of Queen

Elizabeth; besides which, it is one of the polling places for East Gloucestershire. The town and neighbourhood are interesting also to the antiquarian, as having been occupied successively by the Britons, Romans, and West Saxons; nor could the post have been deemed unimportant by the Romans, since three great roads, the Fossway, the Irmin Street, and the Icknield Street, all meet at this point. Scarcely a year passes without the discovery of pavements, statues, coins, and various other vestiges of the Roman occupation. Any description of Cirencester, however, would be very imperfect, that did not include a notice of *Oakley Grove*, the fine seat of Earl Bathurst, a little west of the town. The mansion is in the French style, so commonly adopted at the beginning of the last century, and certainly has little to recommend it. The park, though mostly flat, is pleasingly laid out (chiefly under the direction of the first Lord Bathurst), and comprises some old monuments, not unworthy of a visit.

Beyond this point the nature of the country begins rapidly to change, and the Railway passes through the loveliest cultivated scenery that eye can picture or imagination gaze on:—indeed, such is the charm—the rapid succession of objects in this delightful country, that the eye becomes fairly confused by its richness and magnificence. The Valley of Stroud, indeed, is well known to travellers and tourists, as presenting for many miles a continuous series of lovely landscapes,—so beautiful, indeed, as to remind us of Southey's words:—

> Still bounteous Nature o'er the lovely vale
> Pours forth her gifts profuse; perennial springs
> Flow for her habitants, and genial suns,
> With kindly show'rs, to bless the happy clime
> Combine their gentle influences."

The valley, in fact, assumes almost the character of a mountain-gorge, with a brawling stream in the bottom, which partially forms the motive-power of the numerous cloth and fulling mills of this well known district, and which is often to be seen deeply imbued with the dye used in preparing the cloth. BRIMSCOMBE STATION is somewhat more than 99 miles from Paddington, and 22 miles from Swindon, leading to a town of the same name, actively engaged in weaving woollen cloth;—and about a mile and a half on the south-west is *Minchinhampton*, a considerable town, with about 6,000 inhabitants, built on a hill bordering east on the vale of the Severn, remarkable, like the last mentioned place, for its active industry in weaving woollen cloths.

MILL IN THE STROUD VALLEY.

And now we are approaching the STROUD STATION, and a curious scene presents itself to our view. Indeed, the traveller, as he approaches this station, cannot be otherwise than greatly struck with the singularity of the scenery around him;—the situation of the mills on streams in deep ravines, the scattered and irregular manner in which the houses are built on the hill-sides, as well as the strange contrast between the high land—in many cases either wood or common, very thinly peopled—and the valleys below them studded with houses, and teeming with a busy population.

The parliamentary borough of *Stroud* stands on the side of a hill, close to the Slade or Stroudwater, near its junction with the Froome, and consists principally of a long street, crossed by another at one end, like the letter T, well paved, and lined with good houses. The parish-church is a large and rather handsome structure, with a tower and lofty octagonal steeple at its west end;— the Dissenters, also, have four or five places of worship, and the parish has several school and other charities. It is mainly to the river that Stroud, and the district around it, owes its prosperity; because that stream is not only made available for the working of machinery, but is said to be especially well adapted for the dyeing of scarlet and other colours. The result has been, that the clothing trade has extended itself principally along the banks of the river; along which will be found many fulling mills, &c., very picturesquely situated,—one of which, represented in the previous page, will give a general notion of their appearance.

In fact, the prosperity of the town and district depends almost entirely on the state of the clothing trade, partaking, also, of the fluctuations incident to the latter;—and the trade has of late years been unfavourably affected by the vast improvements in the cloth manufactures of the West-riding of Yorkshire. Power-looms have within the last few years been successfully introduced, and are beginning to meet with favour from the leading manufacturers. Stroud, (which has a population of about 10,000 persons,) was enfranchised by the Reform Bill, which gave it the privilege of sending two members to the British parliament.

The Railway, during the whole of its progress through this singularly beautiful scenery, lies for the most on a steep incline, especially after passing *Sapperton Tunnel*, which cuts through the Coteswold hills before our arrival at Stroud, and is an object of terror (quite groundless) to timid passengers on the up-journey. The Railway, too, is of necessity compelled to follow the sinuous course of the river-valley; whence it abounds in sharp curves, which, in the rapid run down to Gloucester, are very perceptible to the traveller in any fast train, as he will at once feel that first one and then the other side of the carriage is raised to meet the propelling power, and counteract its disposition to run off the rail on the other side of the curve.

THE GLOUCESTER STATION

has the appearance of doing considerable business; but it seems to be a sort of hybrid post, combining the traffic of the two gauge lines, and fully accommodating neither. Nevertheless, the station-accommodations, if not on the most liberal scale, are sufficient for their purpose. And we are now in Gloucester, the " Caer-glow" or fair city of the ancient Britons, the *Glevum* of the Romans, and styled a city, when London itself was but a municipium or borough,—a city, too, that was termed by the venerable Bede, " the noblest of the kingdom." Modern Gloucester stands on an eminence, rising from the Severn at its bifurcation by the Isle of Alney; and the various approaches to the town, embellished with pretty villas, and well-kept pleasure-grounds, fields, orchards, &c., give an air of opulence that is not belied by further examination;—for Gloucester is withal a town and port well-to-do, and looking up in the world. Nevertheless, strange to say, the streets of Gloucester are to this day paved with egg-shaped stones, and without flags; and here and there are many odd-looking houses of the old gable formation, with latticed windows.

The city consists of four principal streets, called Northgate, Eastgate, Southgate, and Westgate, crossing each other at right angles. It possesses some good streets, and well-built substantial houses; but it is ill-paved, though of late years it has been brilliantly lighted with gas. The river, which is here divided into two channels by Alney Island, is crossed by two fine bridges.

There are several handsome public buildings, among which, besides the Cathedral, the Shire Hall, the Tolsey or Town Hall, the County Gaol, and Market House, deserve notice. The *Shire Hall*, in which the assizes and county sessions are held, has a fine front of Ionic architecture, and is well constructed for the purposes of business. The *County Gaol*, built in 1791, at an expense of £35,000, on the site of the old Castle, covers about three acres; it was constructed on a plan suggested by Howard; includes a bridewell and debtors' prison, and has sufficient means for the classification of prisoners. The *Market House*, which is commodious, and of plain exterior, cost £10,000. A spa having been discovered in 1814, a highly ornamented Pump-room and other edifices have been built near it.

Several of the churches are old and handsome structures; the chief of these is the beautiful Cathedral or Abbey Church, occupying one side of College Green, a building 420 feet long by 144 feet broad, built on the site of a former monastery of Benedictines. The present building was partly erected about 1088, but not completed till the close of the fifteenth century; hence it exhibits the various gradations of style during the great era of church architecture, from the Norman conquest downwards. The crypt, the nave, and north aisle, being the oldest parts, are in the Anglo-Norman style, with round, arched windows; the windows of the south aisle, built two centuries later, are of the obtuse lancet shape; while the west front, and the continuation of the nave, erected in the fourteenth century,

exhibit a yet later and more elaborate style than all the rest. Under the tower (which is square, flanked with four highly ornamented pinnacles, and 224 feet high), at the east end of the nave, is the approach to the choir; and from this point is one of the best views of the interior, the highly finished choir, with its curiously wrought roof, forming a remarkable contrast with the simpler architecture of the nave and transepts. The arching of the choir, nave, and transepts is so contrived that, while the eye beholds the massive pillars as they branch upwards, the whole structure has an extraordinary lightness and beauty. The high altar is ornamented with angels playing on musical instruments, and behind it is the great east window, said to be the largest in England, and containing 2,800 square feet of glass. It was set up in the reign of Edward III., and is now much mutilated. The floor in front of the altar is of curiously painted tiles, representing the arms of the Plantagenets, the Earl of Gloucester, &c. A monument of Edward II., near the altar, is well carved, and in good preservation. The choir is 140 feet long, and has 31 stalls on either side, of exquisitely wrought tabernacle work. The lady-chapel, added to the choir in 1228, and rebuilt in 1491, is a peculiarly elegant structure, and most ingeniously united to the church. The cloisters are remarkable for their rich workmanship and beautiful windows; they were begun in 1351, and finished about 1390.

Gloucester was made a bishop's see by Henry VIII. in 1541; but in consequence of the recent ecclesiastical changes, it is now united with Bristol. The churches of St. Mary de Crypt, St. Michael, St. John, and the new one of Christ Church, are all of them edifices ornamental to the town;—besides which there are two very neat district churches newly completed in the suburbs, one at Barton Terrace, and the other at High Orchard, near the Docks. The Wesleyans, Independents, Baptists, Roman Catholics, and others, have also places of worship, and there is a Jews' synagogue. Gloucester has, also, three capital foundation schools, one belonging to the Cathedral, and a Blue-coat School, very well endowed, with a Lancasterian School and a Bell's School, established in 1813 and 1817 respectively. It deserves also to be mentioned, that Sunday schools originated in this city in 1781:—they were first suggested and set on foot by Mr. Raikes, a printer, a benevolent and intelligent individual, who rendered by this act an essential service to humanity.

The trade and prospects of Gloucester are flourishing. It is situated in a fertile and populous district, and enjoys an extensive command of internal navigation. Latterly, also, its importance as a port has been much increased, owing to the facilities given to it by the excavation of the Gloucester and Berkeley Canal, by which the intricate navigation of the Severn is avoided. This canal, opened in 1826, is 18 miles long, commencing at Sharpnesse Point, about two miles and a half from Berkeley, and ending in a commodious basin, a little south of Gloucester; which is 60 feet wide, and, being 18 feet deep, is capable of floating vessels of above 500 tons burden. Gloucester, since the opening of this canal, has had considerable trade with the West Indies and Baltic. The railway between this place and Birmingham is about 50 miles in length, and is a very important line, from its being the direct and only means of communication between the north and west of England, and from its passing through or near several important towns. The manufactures of Gloucester are chiefly confined to the making of pins and needles; but this has declined of late years.

Gloucester has returned two members to the House of Commons since the 23rd of Edward I.; and, previously to the passing of the Reform Act, the franchise was vested in the freemen of the borough, who became so by birth, purchase, or apprenticeship.

At length we have arrived at the CHELTENHAM TERMINUS, somewhat more than 44 miles from Swindon, and 121 miles from London; and a beautiful ride it is all the way from Gloucester, with a fine rich country on either side, with the Cotswold hills directly in front, and the Malvern hills on the extreme left to the north-west. The station is tolerably good; but, considering that it belongs to so important, populous, and wealthy a locality, it scarcely meets the requisitions of the traffic.

CHELTENHAM, aristocratic, beautiful Cheltenham, may boast of a site more lovely than that of any spa in the south of England, except Bath and Clifton;—from both of which, however, it differs in every essential particular. It stands close by a small stream called the *Chelt*, which gives it its name, in the midst of a spacious and fertile plain, open southward and westward, but sheltered from the cold north, east, and south-east winds, by the Malvern hills, and the expansive amphitheatre formed by the meeting of the Cotswold range with the Leckhampton hills, which latter terminate somewhat abruptly about two miles south-east of the town. Cheltenham itself consists principally of one noble and straight avenue, upwards of a mile in length, called the *High Street*, which, though it has still a few old and fifth-rate houses, is lined in many parts with fine ranges of buildings; and it serves, also, as the *point de départ* for a great number of fashionable new streets and squares, which display, in connection with the beauties of cultivated pleasure-land, all the elegant and tasteful varieties of architectural decoration. All the streets and squares within the town are particularly clean, well-paved, and brilliantly lighted with gas. Neither must we forget to take a few strolls into the different suburbs, (especially near *Pittville*,) where will be found in every direction very handsome and picturesque detached villas, surrounded with well-planted pleasure-grounds. Independently, too, of the Spa itself, the agreeableness of the town, from being a sort of *rus in urbe*, (or country brought to town,) and the beauties of the walks and drives in the neighbourhood, the *élite* society of the place offers peculiar attractions to the members of the fashionable world. The town, also, comprises several very handsome and well-appointed hotels, with numerous boarding-houses well conducted, and frequented by genteel company;—besides which, there are libraries, reading-rooms, musical promenades, and all the other adjuncts of a fashionable watering-place. The gentlemen, too, find a healthful amusement during the winter months in hunting with the hounds of Lord Segrave, the Duke of Beaufort, and other packs, that hunt this country.

The parish church of Cheltenham stands near the centre of the town, and is a large edifice of Norman and English architecture, with a nave, choir, and transept, and a central tower rising from the intersection, terminated by a lofty octagonal steeple, visible for many miles round:—a fine rose-window terminates the north transept, and at the east end is a large and very handsome window in the pointed style. The present incumbent, as all the world knows, is the Rev. Francis Close, an extremely valuable clergyman, who has done a vast deal to raise the moral tone of society in Cheltenham; and, as the patronage of the living is in the hands of Simeon's trustees, we are well assured, that it will never be wrongly bestowed in future. Cheltenham has, also, six district churches, most of them—as they should be—in the gift of the incumbent; and perhaps there is no town in England, where the true doctrines of our National church are more faithfully enunciated, than in fashionable Cheltenham. The Roman Catholics have a handsome chapel; and there are ten or twelve places of worship—perhaps more—for various classes of Dissenters; and an Independent chapel has recently been opened, that may fairly compete in architectural taste with any of the churches.

PROPRIETARY COLLEGE, CHELTENHAM.

The above engraving represents a view of the Proprietary College, established on Dodswell Hill, just out of the town. The engraving speaks for the building:—the education and other arrangements are most excellent.

The mineral springs, from which Cheltenham derives its original and chief celebrity, next demand our notice; and our friends must at once understand, that there are several springs, widely differing from one another in chemical and therapeutic qualities. The oldest and first mineral spring was discovered, quite by accident, early in the last century: it is now called the *King's Well;* and about the year 1740 a pump-room, pavilion, promenades, &c., were formed, though in very humble fashion, as compared with the present noble arrangements of modern Cheltenham. To furnish the details of all the springs, and their chemical constituents, can scarcely be considered to enter into the province of a general Guide-book; but reliance may be implicitly placed on Dr. Granville's account of the spa, and the analysis given by him of its numerous springs.

As a place of trade, Cheltenham can offer no claim to notice, except on the score of the business caused by the not insignificant wants of its permanent residents, a considerable number of whom, we believe, are superannuated and very wealthy as well as influential Anglo-Indians, with many others of high family or wealthy means, and impaired constitutions, or else of idle, *insouçiant* habits. Nevertheless, so large a population, amounting now to about 40,000 persons, (one half of whom are either visitors or wealthy residents, keeping establishments,) must be the cause of a large influx of prosperity to the town, and will easily account for the splendid exhibitions of every description of food, from turbot to a red-herring, from prime buck-venison to humble beef and mutton, &c., that may be seen in the markets and shops of Cheltenham.

Cheltenham has to thank the Reform Act for its present privilege of returning *one* member to the House of Commons; and there are about 1,400 registered voters.

And now—after so long and devious a journey through the country traversed by the GREAT WESTERN RAILWAY—we bid our readers farewell. Our task has been accomplished, not, indeed, wholly to our satisfaction; but we hope, at any rate, that enough of real information has been furnished, to serve as a stock on which to engraft more in future editions.

THE END.

EDWARD EGINTON, PRINTER, PLAYHOUSE YARD, LONDON.

REPRODUCED PHOTOLITHO IN GREAT BRITAIN BY J. W. ARROWSMITH LTD, BRISTOL